Peaceful Ways

The Power
of
Making Your Wishes Come True

Peaceful Ways

The Power
of
Making Your Wishes Come True

PIERO FALCI

BOOKS BY PIERO FALCI

Silent Peace Walk

Pay Attention! Be Alert! Discovering Your Route to Happiness

Contact the author at

piero@pierofalci.com

Order additional copies of this book at

https://www.createspace.com/4998041

I like to think of myself as an artist, and my life is my greatest work of art. Every moment is a moment of creation, and each moment of creation contains infinite possibilities.

~ Shakti Gawain

You are never given a wish without also being given the power to make it true.

~ Richard Bach

THANK YOU

Elizabeth Velez, Jaime Arevalo Reyes and Jason Hansra, my teachers, for initiating me in the beautiful teachings of Reiki that so deeply influenced the content of this book. Liz, receive my heartfelt gratitude. Your calm guidance and insightful suggestions certainly made this book better.

Penelope Arango, Maria Elena Penades, Nancy Pflum and Lisa and David Trimble, for helping bring this book to light.

The Mighty 11, for your commitment to never cease of exploring. I am grateful for having you as fellow explorers on this journey.

My dear Peace Walkers, for the inner peace you so diligently cultivate, and for keeping alive the belief that one day the collective consciousness will raise and reveal a just and peaceful world.

My friends at the Back on Track Network, for your selfless service and giving hearts.

Bill Sheehan, my mentor at the Contemplative Outreach and Centering Prayer community, for your gentle guidance and encouragement on my meditative practice.

My Emmaus brothers and sisters, for your resolve to stay on the right road.

Finally, Lu, Pedro and Mateus, the manifestations of Divine Love closest to me, thank you for everything. Thank you for life, love and laughter.

I am profoundly blessed for having all of you in my life.

My mission in life is to unite, and not to divide.
I have been blessed by insights of thinkers who lived throughout
history in many parts of the world.
It is not my intention to promote any one religion or ideology.
Thinkers from all religions and regions of the world inspire me.

CONTENTS

INTRODUCTION

If you are reading this book is because you want a better life. You feel that there is a reason for you to be here on Earth, and you want to fulfill this purpose. You want to give your contribution for the improvement of this world and you want to experience abundance doing it. You want health and happiness, wealth and wisdom, love and peace.

I am here to tell you that if you apply the simple techniques contained in this book regularly – if you make them part of your daily routine -- you will experience fulfillment and serenity. You will love life, be abundantly blessed, and be a blessing to the Universe.

I am here to talk to you about meditation, visualization and affirmation, three simple techniques that will help you clear your mind, uncover your highest purpose, envision the life of your dreams, and allow this vision to become your reality.

What you are about to learn here is not new; it is part of the wisdom of the ages that has always been available to us. You may be surprised with what I am going to say but, in a way, we all meditate, visualize and affirm already. Everyday we have countless moments of meditation, visualization and affirmation. Unfortunately, the majority of these activities are happening unconsciously, without proper thought and purpose. Therefore, they are not working to produce the best results. In fact, if negative thoughts and emotions are being projected, they may be damaging you and the world around you.

So, the first thing I want you to understand is that what I am going to share in this book is not new for you. The second thing is that the techniques presented here are very, very simple; what I am going to present is not complicated at all. Be aware that, in a way, you already know how to meditate, visualize and affirm, because we all do these things naturally. Be happy, then, because there's no need for a big effort to learn these techniques. All you will have to do is to learn to practice them consciously and purposefully in order to produce the best outcomes.

Again, be happy because it's easy.

As you read this book you will see that I don't believe it is necessary to work extremely hard or follow strict rules to achieve our goals. This is something that I believed in the past, but that I don't accept as true anymore. I believe in what Deepak Chopra calls "the law of least effort," which states that as long as we are living in accordance with a greater universal plan and allowing ourselves to be who we are meant to be, the desired results will spontaneously come to life; things will manifest themselves easily, at the right time. If not -- if too much effort is needed -- then we should question our goals. Meditation, creative visualization, and positive affirmations are techniques that help us realize who we are meant to be, allowing us to live the grand lives we are meant to live.

Since we are creators by nature, I believe we are called to take action. I believe we are called to take thoughtful, focused action, the kind of action that contributes to the natural unfolding of life. I believe in flowing with the stream of life instead of desperately swimming against it. More than working hard to produce results, I believe in removing self-imposed obstacles that prevent the desired results to manifest.

Let us reflect upon our understanding of effort, time and outcome. We have learned that effort applied over time produces results. This is true and undeniable. We also have learned that if we increase our efforts and put in more time, we will produce bigger and better outcomes. This is questionable.

Have you noticed that some people work very hard, for extended periods of time, and produce timid results, while others, without applying themselves half as hard produce extraordinary results in no time? There is more to the equation of achieving than action alone.

Those who produce extraordinary results in short time and without great efforts are the ones connected with the Source. They don't waste energy doing what they have not been called to do. They pursue their vocations, doing what they like and liking what they do. Their days are full of activities that make them feel good. They don't waste energy pretending to be who they are not. They are authentic. Love Energy flows easily through them.

This is a key point of what I want to share with you in this book: more than learning, acquiring, or adding anything, I want you to focus on removing. More than struggling in life, I want you to focus on what comes easy and makes you feel good. More than developing yourself in order to be someone else, I want you to focus on removing all the things that are preventing you from being you.

Did you get this?

I believe that at our core we already are who we are meant to be. What we have to do is to allow that being to come to light. I believe in removing internal blocks and allowing Love -- the Universal Intelligence -- to flow freely through us and to work in us to manifest the wonderful beings we were brought here to be. My intention in this book is to show you tools that you can use to remove those obstacles.

So here is the good news again. And I am going to repeat this because it is extremely important.

At your core, you already are who you are meant to be: a marvelous being!

Now, get out of the way and allow that splendid being to come to life.

Stop putting obstacles and preventing your highest self to emerge.

Remove your doubts, fears and self-imposed limitations.

Allow The Energy to flow freely through you.

Allow your grandest self to rise.

Allow yourself to give the wonderful contributions to humanity that only you can give.

Allow yourself to be the best that you can be.

Allow yourself to enjoy a brilliant and joyful life.

Allow.

Piero Falci

<><><>

CHAPTER ONE

REST

"Come to me, all of you who are weary and heavy-laden, and I will give you rest." ~ Jesus

Before we talk about anything else, let us talk about rest. That's how I want to begin. I want to begin this book talking about rest.

Don't you find interesting that among all the countless things that Jesus could offer us, he is offering us *rest*?

I honestly think that we don't give ourselves enough rest. If you are like me, the idea of taking time off to rest, leaving the 'must-dos' for later, has always been very difficult to accept.

You see, many of us wake up in the morning with an alarm clock and spend our entire days in a state of alarm. We don't relax a single moment. We get up, get dressed and get going. We wake up in the morning telling ourselves, "I have to do this and I have to do that." We create those long and unrealistic to-do lists, with too many things to do and not enough time to do them. Then we go through our days rushing and running, collecting all the scattered pieces of our lives and trying to put them together. We go through our days thinking about what we have to do next instead of concentrating on what we have in front of us, be it the work at hand, or the person we may be with. Most of the time, we are not here, now; our minds are elsewhere and 'elsewhen.' We are not enjoying the present.

And as it invariably happens, unexpected things pop up, and there goes the plan we had for the day. When this happens, we immediately tense up. Instead of giving thanks for the unexpected, and accepting what the Forces of the Universe have brought to us, we react against them. We don't surrender and look for the good and the beauty in the unexpected. We decide not to go with the flow, but to swim against it. As a result, irritation, impatience, frustration, worry, anger and anxiety become our companions for the day. And at the end of the day, when we review our to-do list, we tell ourselves, "I have not done this. I have not done that. I should have done this. I could have done that. I am not good enough. I am worthless." And we go to bed feeling tired, guilty and defeated.

Is this your life? Now let me ask you this: What kind of life is this? Why are you going to go through life feeling this way: tired, guilty and defeated? Can't you see that you are the one imposing too many demands on your own self? Can't you see that you are the one judging and condemning your own self? Can't you see that you are the one creating your own stress, the biggest killer of all?

Yes, we begin our days with our plans, and we may end up doing something completely different. I am here to tell you that this is OK. The Spirit leads us to do what the Spirit wants us to do. We have to accept. We have to surrender. We have to relax. We have to breathe deeply, reconvene, recollect, and be gentle with ourselves. We have to find joy in whatever is brought to us. At the end of the day, instead of focusing on what we have not done and feeling guilty and defeated, we shall focus on the much that we have accomplished and feel victorious.

How can we do this?

I suggest you use the reframing technique. Reframe your thoughts and emotions. Rewrite the script. Instead of telling a negative story, tell a positive one. Focus on all the positive facts and aspects of the day and tell a tale of victory and gratitude. "I had a fantastic day, full of unexpected occurrences and new opportunities. I took action and I am moving closer to my goals. I gave a great contribution to the world today!" No more negative stories. No more *shouldas, couldas,* and guilty feelings. Tell yourself, "It was a glorious day. I am grateful for everything that happened and everything that was given to me. And I am moving on; the past is gone."

Besides creating "to-do" lists, I would like to encourage you to also create "it-is-done" lists. List all the many things you have already done and have already accomplished, not only what you have done today, but all that you have accomplished throughout your life. Review those lists and feel good!

Many times we struggle to get a lot of things done in order to make our wishes come true. It would be better to simply surrender and let the Universe take care of the details. We should learn to let go and let God. One good practice is to read this note every morning:

Good morning.
Here is God.
I will be handling all your problems and concerns today.
I will not require your help.
So relax and enjoy the day.
Have fun.
I love you.
God.

I am sure you got it, didn't you?

So let us review what we have seen so far.
1 - You don't have to be productive and concerned with producing results all the time.
2 - You don't have to worry all the time.
3 - You don't have to feel unworthy, or guilty, if you have not produced what you set yourself up to.

Pause and breathe. Give yourself rest. Exercise your birthright. Exercise your right to rest. I am here to tell you that it is OK for you to do so. Why? Because resting is important.

It is in the moments of rest that we become aware of the magnificent being that resides within us, and how we have been covering it with layers that prevent it to come to the light.

Rest allows us to become aware of this magnificent being – the grandest version of ourselves – and of the many obstacles we have placed on its way for it to manifest itself.

Moments of rest allow us to feel how the Intelligent Energy is flowing through us and how blockages are being gently removed for it to flow more freely. This awareness – brought to us through rest – allows us to take the most effective actions to remove the blocks.

Rest allows us to figure out what is most important, and focus on the activities through which we can give our greatest contributions to humanity.

Rest prepares us to take the action needed to manifest our highest selves.

Finally, rest teaches us to be in the present and enjoy it.

Through daily practice, you will learn to allow yourself to rest. I hope you give yourself time to rest everyday. I would like you to feel that the time you take for meditation, creative visualization and positive affirmations is a time of rest. I would like you to realize the times you take to do the things you really enjoy doing are times of rest. I would like you to realize how this time of rest will, in fact, make you more productive. Rest will make you produce the results that will really make you happy.

Now that we have understood why we should not be worried about being productive all the time, and have taken in the benefits of resting, we are ready to give ourselves permission to take time to meditate, visualize and affirm. And this is what we will cover next in this book.

CHAPTER TWO

MEDITATION

"All men's miseries derive from not being able to sit in a quiet room alone." ~
Blaise Pascal

We just reviewed the benefits of resting. How is this connected with meditation? Well, meditation is resting for the mind. It is through meditation that we come to the quiet center of our beings where, in the silence, we listen. It is there that we find the best answers for all our questions. It is there that we find the wisdom that produces joy and peace. Meditation is taking time off from thinking, planning, worrying and judging, and giving our minds some rest. Our decision to give ourselves permission to take time to meditate is where the entire process of meditation begins.

You see, we are always busy thinking. It seems that we always have something to do and somewhere to go. Well, meditation invites us to think less about what we have to do and where we have to go, so we can be more in the here-now. Meditation is a time when we become the observers of the activity that goes inside our brains. We observe our thoughts but, to the best of our ability, we do not engage with them.

This is important, so let me repeat this one more time: you begin your meditation grounded on the decision of not engaging with your thoughts.

The whole process of meditation is a process of non-engagement, of acknowledging your thoughts but letting them go without further analyzing them, without starting a conversation in your head.

What do I mean by non-engagement?

I mean that you do not allow one thought to bring about a series of other thoughts. You don't allow the troubling emotion that one thought may bring up to open the gates for a flood of other upsetting emotions to emerge. For instance, you don't allow one worry to bring about other worries that will block the connection with the Source and the free flow of the stream of Energy. And you do all this in a very gentle way. You are not fighting against your thoughts, trying to subjugate them to your will, nor are you trying to chase them away. Meditation is not you struggling against your thoughts. Meditation is an expression of extreme gentleness with oneself. Meditation is a time of rest. It is a joyful time of tranquility. It is the time you give yourself to re-energize and return to a balanced state. So take this time and be kind with yourself.

Meditation is easy. It is a process of acknowledgment and release. You simply become aware of what you are thinking and feeling and, in that same moment, you gently release those thoughts, feelings and emotions. It is a process of catching and letting go that you do over and over again. It could also be said that meditation is a process of non-catching your thoughts, of simply allowing them to flow away. And, as I said, this is to be done with extreme gentleness. So, be gentle with your thoughts. Allow them to be there without fighting with them. Greet them with a gentle peace, and allow them to pass through.

Where and when to meditate should be thoughtfully considered.

A calm and silent environment to meditate is important. I recommend meditating first thing in the morning, immediately after waking up, before the activities and demands of the day kick in. If necessary, leave your bed before everyone else in your household does, and find a place where you will not be disturbed. Sit down in a comfortable position, with both feet flat on the ground, and hands resting on your lap. Try to keep your back straight. If necessary put a pillow between your back and the back of the chair.

This being said… feel free to ignore everything I have just told you.

Are you still sitting, or did you fall off your chair?

You know, I am not that rigid, strict teacher. I favor experimentation, exploration, and hands-on learning. For me, trial and error works. So, experiment meditating in the sitting position I described above, but if after trying for a while you feel that that position is not good for you, simply find the position that is more comfortable to you, whatever it may be. For instance, it really doesn't matter if you have your feet on the ground or not, or if you are sitting in a lotus position, or if the palms of your hands are facing up or down. Since you will not be moving for quite some time, just find a position that is comfortable for you. Why? Because you want to avoid tensions in your body from distracting you.

And then, what do you do next?

Well, begin by closing your eyes, and inviting Love to flow freely through you. I will be talking more about the free flow of Love later in this book, but for now, just think about Love flowing through your body, freely, without any obstacles. Then, observe your breath.

Let me open a parenthesis here: One of the most common ways used to enter a meditative state is to engage in a repetitive behavior, such as focusing on breathing or repeating a phrase or mantra. I will briefly describe both and through practice you will find what works for you. Close parenthesis.

Just observe your breath. Don't try to modify it. Just feel the air flowing in and out. As you do this, you will feel the desire to take deeper breaths. Go ahead and do it. Observe how, with each inhalation and exhalation, you feel calmer and calmer. This in itself is a form of meditation. When you get distracted by noises, sensations, or thoughts, go back to observing your breath and feel how it calms you down. This coming back to observing your breathing is what will help you not to engage with what may be trying to catch your attention and distract you.

Another way o meditate, probably the most common, is by employing a mantra. Most commonly, mantra is a word, but it can be a mere sound, a syllable, or a group of words. The literal translation of mantra is "instrument of thought." Mantra, therefore, should be understood as a tool to help us with our thoughts during our meditations. We choose our mantra before meditating. In Centering Prayer, one of the forms of meditation that I practice, the mantra is called "the sacred word." You are invited to treat the sacred word with reverence, but you may decide not to; it is up to you. Sometimes the mantra is reverently handed down in some form of ritual, but this is not necessary. Listen to your inner self and choose your own mantra. Use it for as long as you like and if you find another one to be more meaningful for you, do not hesitate to adopt it.

Now that you have a mantra, how do you use it?

Here's how. When, during meditation, you realize that your mind is drifting away, when you realize that you are engaging with your thoughts, when you catch yourself having a conversation in your head, simply pause, acknowledge what may be going on, and then silently recite the mantra. That's all. The mere act of bringing the mantra to your consciousness gently sends out the instruction to stop the inner dialogue and not engage with the thoughts. As you silently recite the mantra you gently let whatever may be distracting you go. Note that I said gently. Centering Prayer places a great emphasis on gentleness. That method instructs us to "introduce the sacred word inwardly as gently as laying a feather on a piece of absorbent cotton." It can't be any gentler than that, right?

Now, you can also use images to help you not engage with your thoughts. For instance: imagine that you are standing on the side of a river and boats are passing by. Each boat carries a thought. The thought may be about a situation that you are living right now, or something that you have to do, or an event in your past. Since those thoughts are attracting you, you may feel tempted to jump into the boats. Well, refrain from doing that. Remain on the margin as an observer. Let the boats go by. As you let them go they become rarer and rarer, until there will be very few of them, or none at all.

Another way of utilizing images to manage your thoughts is to envision a sky. Attach your thoughts to the clouds that are passing by, and relax knowing that the clouds are now carrying your thoughts away. Your thoughts, just like the clouds, are dissolving and disappearing. See the sky becoming clearer and clearer. As time goes by, envision a completely clear sky.

I encourage you to use these images or any other that you may come up with and that you feel will work for you.

OK. That's all. You now know the basics of meditation. Isn't it simple?

There's a lot more to be said about meditation and how to do it, but it is not my intention to do it in this book. There are many great resources out there to help you learn and support your meditation practice, and I have listed some of them at the end of this book.

What I have described above is what could be called formal meditation. But there are many other less structured forms of meditating. You can take part in a guided meditation where a facilitator guides you through it. Many times the instructor will use guided meditation to bring your body to a state of great relaxation. He or she will guide you to direct your attention to each part of your body, and consciously relax it completely. You can actually meditate in any body position, anywhere, and at any time: inside your car in the parking lot, during your bus ride, on your airplane seat, laying on a couch, watching the sunrise, and so on. I like to meditate listening to soothing music. "Sanctuary" by George Skaroulis and "Light from Assisi" by Richard Shulman are two CDs that I play over and over again during my meditations; I just love them. You can meditate while watching a slide show or a movie with beautiful photos or visuals created by artists. Consider, for instance, a visit to a museum; it can be a great opportunity to look at art and practice a less structured form of meditation. I particularly like the Silent Peace Walks at daybreak, a way of practicing meditation while walking in silence through nature. As you can see, since meditation is an inner exercise, it can be practiced anywhere. It can be integrated with many other activities. For instance, Yoga and Reiki are very conducive to meditation and inner peace. The same can be said about the calm setting of any house of worship; churches, synagogues, mosques, temples invite us to go to our inner room where we connect, communicate and commune with the Divine Mystery and experience inner-peace.

I recommend that you practice formal meditation for 20 minutes at a time, twice a day, morning and evening. But if you feel that you can't do that, practice it for any amount of time. Even one minute of going to the center of your being brings great benefits.

Don't expect something extraordinary to happen during formal meditation. It may happen and if it does, rejoice. But that is not the objective. Actually there are no objectives. You are not trying to reach any goal except giving your mind some rest.

Just think for a moment about those times when you are trying to solve a problem and you can't find a solution. Can you remember those instances when you finally stop thinking about the problem, start doing something else, and the solution spontaneously pops up? Haven't you had such experiences? I call them my Shower Moments, only because many times solutions unexpectedly come up to me while I am showering. Well, you may have plenty of shower moments during your meditation. You may come up with great ideas. But let me encourage you to release them as well. Let them go. Let all thoughts go. No matter how good they may be. Let them all go, both the bad and the good ones. Trust me when I tell you that those great ideas will come back to you later. But now is not the time to entertain them. Now it is time for you to give your mind some rest.

One more thing: be gentle with yourself and your meditation practice. Do not judge the quality of your meditation. No one is evaluating your performance, so do not put that burden on you. Do not put yourself down for not being able to meditate as you think you should. Do not judge and condemn yourself. Stick with the decision of being gentle with yourself and continue meditating. Each one of us is different, and each person will have a different experience with meditation.

I want you to trust me when I say that meditation is one of the safest and healthiest things you can do. This being said, I want to make you aware that, especially in the beginning, meditation can be uncomfortable and even scary. For those who have never meditated before, even one minute of silence can feel like an unbearable eternity. The moment you become conscious of the agitation and the torrent of thoughts that are going through your head, you feel the desire to stop and get out. As you meditate, emotions that you have long suppressed begin to emerge. You go through a process called "emotional unloading." You feel overwhelmed, having to deal with much more than what you think you can handle. Well, you are not given what you cannot handle. Fear is part of the process, and I assure you that if you stick with it you will start reaping the fabulous benefits that meditation produces.

The interesting paradox is that although meditation is resting, in order for you to reach a restful state you may experience some unrest. Some work is necessary, especially in the beginning. So, it could also be said that meditation is a fitness workout for a healthy, tranquil mind. Just like a physical workout, you have to go through some pain in order to experience some gain.

The practice of meditation leads us to be more mindful, to live more and more in the present moment. Once we start the meditative practice, we begin to pay more attention to our own selves and the world around us. As we practice living mindfully, we begin seeing beauty that we didn't see before. We become better observers of our emotions, even in the moments when we are not formally meditating, and this allows us to make better choices of thoughts, words and actions, which bring about more peaceful and fulfilling existences. We become capable of better sorting things out. This leads us to concentrate our energy on the positive contributions we can offer instead of wasting our time and energy with things that are not important, or with things that we cannot control.

For me, the greatest benefit of meditation is bringing the learned technique of thought-scanning to those other moments of life when we are not formally meditating. By paying more attention, by being more alert, you become a better observer of what is going on, both outside and inside your own self. You find yourself more and more in the present moment: here, now. You stay in a mindful state throughout the day. This practice is called mindfulness, or mindful living, or living a contemplative life. If you want to reap the benefits, stay as the witness, the observer, the one who is detached and scrutinizes thoughts and moods. Ask yourself, "What am I feeling right now?" and choose to feel good. A good life is a life full of feel good moments.

Why is meditation important?

Meditation is important because it pacifies our minds, shows us infinite possibilities, reveals our highest purposes, and makes us aware of the power we already have to make our wishes come true. Meditation is important because it restores the natural balance of our organisms. It stops the habitual train of thoughts and takes us from the lower realm where we spend the majority of our time to a higher level of consciousness where we begin to see and feel different. We experience an expansion of understanding. We see new possibilities. We feel our potential.

Our wishes will come true when our thoughts allow them to come true. This is important. As a man thinks in his heart, so is he. If you want your wishes to come true you must think and feel that they are possible, that they are for the highest good, that you deserve the rewards that they will bring, that they are inevitable, and that it is your destiny to manifest them.

CHAPTER THREE

THE PEACEFUL WAYS METHOD
OF
MAKING WISHES COME TRUE

Before we go any further, I want to talk briefly about the method presented in this book. This process of manifesting your dreams starts with removing the clutter and uncovering who you really are, and Meditation is extremely important during this first phase. Actually, as you will see, Meditation is extremely helpful during all phases of the process. Once you have achieved some clarity about who you are and what your highest calling in life is, you will move on to the goal-setting phase. Once you have defined your goals, you will apply Meditation, Creative Visualization and Positive Affirmations to help you achieve them. Finally, by applying the Just For Today – JFT -- technique you will revisit your goals and take action everyday, which will assure success.

Now, in order to properly define your goals, you should first meditate. I recommend you do so focusing on the following five areas:
1. giving thanks
2. letting go of fear and worries
3. letting go of anger
4. being honest and authentic
5. being kind

I will talk extensively about each one of these mental exercises later on in this book, but for the sake of understanding the power of this sequence let me elaborate just a bit. First, let me tell you that this sequence is based on the Five Reiki Precepts. Reiki is a healing practice originated in Japan that believes in the existence of a Life Force that runs through all things. Many names have been given to this Force. People from different regions of the world and throughout history have named it Ki, Ch'i, Qi, Prana, Pneuma, Mana, Ruah, The Holy Spirit, Soul, etc. We may call it Love. According to the teachings, when the Life Energy is running freely, things are OK, but not so when it meets an obstacle that prevents its free flow. Well, Reiki teaches us that as we go through life, our lack of gratitude, our fears and worries, our ill feelings toward others and ourselves, our lack of honesty and authenticity, and our selfishness place a series of blocks that prevent the free flow of Love. Reiki is a healing practice that teaches us how to remove these obstacles, and one of the practices of achieving this goal is to meditate on the five precepts.

This sequence of five meditations begins with you recognizing the wonderful life you have and giving thanks for it. You will express gratitude for what has been given to you already. And it is important for this to be your starting point. You have to make an inventory of what you have, before putting yourself in motion to get more. You have to recognize where you are before you set yourself in motion to go elsewhere.

Then, by focusing on the positive aspects of your life, you will be able to dispel the negative emotions brought up by fear. You will then practice to release anger and other negative feelings toward other individuals. Imagine for a moment that you are moving to a new and better house and that you are getting rid of stuff that does not serve you anymore. Well, in order to make the most out of the next phase – the goal-setting phase -- you have to gently release what is holding you back so you may arrive at this new phase as light as possible. Why? Because it is during the goal-setting phase that you will be imagining your future life. You want to do this activity feeling free, light, and open to all possibilities.

As you meditate deeply on who you are and what is the highest contribution you can offer, you will develop the commitment to be completely authentic and honest with yourself. By doing so, you will feel the enormous power that allows you to make your dreams come true.

Finally you will bring to your mind thoughts of kindness and generosity which will make your passage here on Earth much more meaningful and enjoyable. You will focus not so much on what you want to get, but on the gifts that you can give.

OK. Now that we have gone through the healthiest goal-setting process that I know, we are called to apply the Guided Meditations, Creative Visualizations and Positive Affirmations techniques everyday to make sure we achieve the life-changing goals we set for ourselves.

Guided Meditations, Creative Visualizations and Positive Affirmations are powerful methods that populate our minds with positive thoughts which help us manifest our dreams.

These techniques help us release the negative thoughts and take us to think positively and optimistically.

As we get better at scanning our thoughts, it will be easier for us to let the negative ones go and bring more of the positive ones to our minds. With practice we will experience a progressive reduction in the emergence of worry, fear and anger, and we will get better and better at gently replacing pessimism with optimism.

In order to help you make your wishes come true, I will guide you through the sequence of guided meditations, creative visualizations and positive affirmations that will enhance your confidence in possibilities, potential and positive outcomes.

You will find material to support this process in the second part of the book, but right now let us discuss some of the important elements of our method in the next chapters.

Let us talk about:

1 – Letting go

2 – Setting goals

3 – Creative Visualization

4 – Positive Affirmations

5 – The JFT Technique

CHAPTER FOUR

LETTING GO

As we have seen, we start this whole process by giving thanks for who we are, for what was given to us, and for what is coming our way.

The second step on this journey is letting go of what is holding us back. And I have chosen to present this step in more detail just because what I call "cleaning up, or removing the clutter, or removing the obstacles that prevent Love from flowing freely" is extremely important for the success of the following step of knowing your purpose in life and setting goals accordingly.

So, get ready. This is a time to let go of the things you don't want to experience in your life anymore. Let go of the things you believe do not serve the Highest Good. Let go of the things that are holding you back. Let go of the things that are not helping you. Let go of the things that are blocking the free flow of Love Energy through you.

How do we identify these things? Well, you already know what these things are. You may have buried them, but now you have an opportunity to release them.

How do you do it? Well, revisit your life. Remember the experiences you had. Remember coming into this world and being loved. See yourself as a newborn, a toddler, a child, a teenager, a young adult, and so on. Bring to your mind the happy moments, and be grateful. Treasure these memories.

After doing this, remember the not so happy moments. Give thanks for the adversities. Give thanks, forgive others and forgive yourself. Think about your worries, your fears. Think about those who made you angry. Decide that you will not carry this load any longer with you. See yourself releasing what does not serve you anymore. See yourself throwing all those things away.

During this "Letting Go" stage authenticity and honesty with oneself is of the utmost importance.

Maybe you are not doing what you have been summoned by the Universe to do.

Maybe you are not living the life you are supposed to live.

Maybe you are clinging to a life that does not serve you anymore. If so, it is time to let go.

Be honest. Be authentic.

In life, some things must die, in order for new things to be born.

Maybe it is time for you to allow your old life, your old self, your old persona to die so you can manifest the new you.

No death, no transformation. No death, no change. No death, no birth.

THE BURNING BOWL CEREMONY

The Burning Bowl Ceremony is a ritual of releasing those things that do not serve the Highest Good any longer. You are called to write down on a piece of paper those things you don't want in your life and then burn that paper in the purifying flames.

Take advantage of this ceremony. Choose to be silent and to treat it with reverence and respect. Burn the papers where you have written what you want to cast off. Tell yourself that fire will consume those things forever. Burn your sorrows, your pains, your sufferings. Burn your grief and sadness. Burn you fears, worries, doubts and anxiety. Burn your anger, rage and hatred. Burn them all. Let go and let God. Feel that they are gone now. Feel that you have put them behind, once and for all. Feel that you have been forgiven. Feel that you have forgiven. Feel that what you have released is forever gone and will not trouble you anymore. You have unburdened yourself. Feel relieved and renewed. Feel how good you feel now. The load is gone and you feel light. You feel that you can fly.

Now that you let go of all the heavy load that was holding you back -- now that you feel light and free -- is the right time for you to go to a higher ground and see new possibilities for you and the life ahead of you.

Now that you feel powerful is the right time for you to allow your authentic you to come to life.

CHAPTER FIVE

SETTING GOALS

We shall not cease from exploration
And the end of all our exploring
Will be to arrive where we started
And know the place for the first time.
~ T. S. Eliot

We have now arrived at the goal-setting phase. But before we dive in, let us reflect on The Hero's Journey.

Joseph Campbell was a mythologist who did a wonderful job researching rituals, traditions and stories from all over the world. According to his findings, all of us, throughout the ages, have been basically telling the same story -- situations and characters may change, but the stories are the same. The recurring stories and archetypes apparently rise from a common source within all of us that many refer to as "the collective unconscious." He made us see that that all mythic narratives are variations of a single great story, which with time came to be known as The Hero's Journey.

What Joseph Campbell did was to identify and organize the elements of the great mythic stories. Some of these elements are "The Call to Adventure, The Refusal to Take the Call, The Departure, The Initiation, The Quest, and The Return." His work is fascinating. I encourage you to learn more about Joseph Campbell, and for that I highly recommend the documentary *"Finding Joe"* by Pat Solomon, a wonderful example of masterfully crafted filmmaking.

The Hero's Journey is the great myth. And why are myths important?

Life is a journey that calls us to deal with the great mysteries of existence, and myths are important because they, in a way, describe the adventure of life and provide helpful clues for our own journeys. This journey begins with the suspicion that we are more than mere animals with sophisticated brains and may lead us to realize that we are, as Teilhard de Chardin said, *"spiritual beings having human experiences."* Myths help us deal with the mystery. Myths allow us to learn about ourselves so we can thrive. Myths encourage us to live the life we were given, find the deeper meaning of our lives, our authentic selves, our untapped potential, our place in the world, where we are on our journeys, what we are being called to do, and the enormous power we have. Myths help us understand that we must accept the Call to Adventure. Myths help us get to that sacred place within our own selves where we unlock our creative powers in order to perform magnificent feats.

The Hero's Journey is the journey each one of us has to undertake to get rid of all the limiting beliefs, fears, doubts, masks, and reveal our authentic selves to the world. It is the journey in which we battle our lowest selves to become the grandest versions of ourselves. The most heroic of all acts is to discover who we are, and who we are meant to be. It takes great courage to follow our bliss and live the lives we were brought here to live.

And how we do this?

By being ourselves. By being authentic and manifesting your highest selves.

Unfortunately, we don't do this. We avoid risks. We play it safe. We conform to the expectations and demands of others and we end up living mediocre lives.

I am here to tell you that the most important thing you can do in your life is to discover who you are meant to be and do what you are called to do. Follow your bliss. Accept the Call to Adventure. Face your fears and doubts and overcome them. Don't pay attention to the voices that tell you not to do it, that you will fail, that you are not prepared for the challenge, that you should postpone your journey for sometime in the future when conditions may be better. Put yourself in motion and helpers will show up. Mentors, teachers, guides, instructors, messengers, angels, they will all come to help you.

Follow your bliss... now. If not now, when? If not you, who? The time is now and you are the one.

"Follow your bliss
and the Universe will open doors for you
where there were only walls."
~ Joseph Campbell

Education is great when it instills self-confidence and expands a person's horizons, but it is bad when it instills fear and restricts people's aspirations. Good education is the one that encourages individuals to follow their bliss. Bad education is the one that tells individuals to conform and play safe. Good education is the one that teaches that one should never cease from exploring because there will always be several answers to the same question. Poor education is the one that teaches that there is only one answer, the one people in positions of authority hand down and demand to be accepted without questioning. This kind of education leaves you stuck.

Now consider that movement is an attribute of life and stagnation is a characteristic of death. I would like to encourage you to seek life and movement. In this context, I encourage you to examine your beliefs. Remember what Socrates said: *"The unexamined life is not worth living."* Go ahead and examine life. Investigate. Ask questions. Explore. Consider new possibilities. Consciously unlearn the limiting viewpoints that you have unconsciously learned and that do not serve you any longer. Put everything that limits you aside. Let go of the old beliefs that do not allow you to move forward and live the extraordinary life you where brought here to live.

Why am I mentioning the Hero's Journey in this book? Because that is what is really important in life: to do what we have been called to do. To do what we do best. To put our unique combination of talents to work in order to produce the unique gifts that only we can produce so we can give our highest contributions to the world.

In the goal-setting process that I am describing, you are being called to find out what is calling you. So, listen. You must answer that call. Do must not let your calling in life pass you by.

THE GOAL-SETTING TECHNIQUE

Let us step back now and return to the end of the Burning Bowl Ceremony. You have released your burden and you feel light. You imagine yourself going for a flight. From above you can see an open field displaying infinite possibilities for yourself. You feel that you are free to choose whatever you want. You feel that the power of the Universe will bring what you want to you. You feel connected with that power. You feel it flowing feely through you. Possibilities are boundless and everything is possible. Nothing is impossible. Not even the sky is the limit. There are no limits.

So now is the time to meditate. I suggest you meditate on the 4 questions presented by Wayne Muller in his book, *How Then, Shall We Live? Four Simple Questions that Reveal the Beauty and Meaning of Our Lives.* Take your time and reflect…

1. Who am I?
2. What do I love?
3. How do I live knowing that I will die?
4. What is my gift to the family of the Earth?

Through these simple questions you see the preciousness of your human life, and the unique gifts you have to offer the world. When you meditate upon these questions, you figure out who you really are and who you want to be. You awaken in you the courage and wisdom that allow you to break free and go beyond what you once considered possible.

Who am I? What is the purpose for my existence? What is calling me? What does God want from me?

The truth is that if you do not pursue your highest calling, you will never be completely happy. So take your time to find out what your mission in life is, and set goals that are in accordance.

We all have questions about where we are headed, and what our purpose in life is. Let us be gentle and create spaces for the answers to emerge. Meditation assists us in clearing the channels that allow us to listen to the answers coming from within. It also helps us be more attentive and receptive to the guidance that comes from without.

Now, if you don't yet have it clear what your purpose in life is, go with your intuition. What is your gut telling you now? What do you want for your life in the upcoming year? Think about your body, your mind, your heart and your soul. What do you want for you in the physical, mental, emotional, and spiritual realms? What are your professional and financial aspirations? What kind of relationships are you seeking? How do you want to live? Where? What do you want to do? What do you want to have? Who do you want to share your experiences with? You may want a new car, a new job, or a partner who loves and cares for you. Whatever you want is OK. At this stage, don't judge your desire. Feel free to write down what you want.

Write your goals in a positive, affirmative, confident, decisive, optimistic way. Look at your future, imagine your ideal life, and write down who you are, what you do, and what you have. Here are some examples:
1 - "In my ideal life I own and live in a condo by the beach and watch the sunrise every morning."
2 - "In my ideal life I own and drive a brand new sports car that brings me lots of joy."
3 - "In my ideal life I meditate, visualize and affirm everyday."

4 - "In my ideal life I live mindfully, scanning thoughts, moods and occurrences and making healthy choices that bring me joy and peace."

At this point, your job is to visualize the life you want. Let the Universe worry about how you are going to get what you want. Do not worry with the "how." Concentrate on what you want. See it. Feel it. Feel that you deserve it. Say to yourself, "The Universe is bringing me all that I visualize, or more. I will receive the things I desire, or even better things."

Harmony with the Universe is very important in fulfilling our desires. We must remember that we cannot manifest anything solely through our own efforts, but we can remove obstacles and allow the free flow of Love through us. When we harmonize with the Universe, our desires become one with the desires of the Universe. Then all we have to do is to allow the Creative Force to flow through us and bring those desires to light. When we meditate we connect with the Energy of the Universe. When we visualize we create the blueprint of what we want and hand it over to the One who will build and deliver it to us. When we are in harmony with the Universal Energy conditions are in place for our desires to manifest effortlessly.

OK, now that you climbed from a lower level, with all its self-imposed limitations, to a higher level from where you can see all the possibilities, it is time to bring in the technique of creative visualization. And that is what we will cover in the next chapter.

CHAPTER SIX

CREATIVE VISUALIZATION

"Imagination is the preview of life's coming attractions"
~ Albert Einstein

It is time to create images. You can create mental images, but you can also create actual images such as drawings, paintings, collages, photos, slide shows and movies. Going back to your images will remind you of the great life you will soon be living. This will make you feel good.

Everybody imagines, dreams and visualizes. We all do those things – naturally, unconsciously -- all the time. Daydreaming is visualizing, but it is visualizing without purpose. Creative Visualization, the one we will be talking about here, is dreaming with the intention of making dreams come true; it is imagining with the purpose of manifesting what is being imagined.

Our thoughts create our reality. Thoughts bring about things. Just look around. Everything that was created by men was first imagined. If you want to create a better life, you have to imagine it, dream it, visualize it, and feel it… vividly.

Images are powerful. What you visualize materializes. What you visualize you attract. Think of yourself as a magnet that attracts what you visualize. You attract to your life those things and situations you think about the most, the ones you energize with feelings and emotions. You become what you think about the most. Thoughts become things.

That's why we must be careful with our thoughts because as a man thinks in his heart, so is he. Good thoughts will manifest good things while negative thoughts will bring about the inverse. Move your focus away from what you don't want -- the things you want to avoid, the things you don't want to happen, the things you are afraid of -- to all the good things and situations you want in your life. That's where your focus should be. The more you populate your days with good thoughts, the more you will attract positive people, events and circumstances into your life. Mind shapes reality. Treat yourself as you would like to be treated. Treat yourself poorly, and others will do the same. Give yourself a royal treatment, and others will treat you like royalty.

Observe your feelings and emotions. Gently replace the negative with positive ones. Whatever you are feeling today is creating your tomorrow. Listen to the Universe. It is telling you, "Your wish is my command." Feel healthy, happy, and prosperous. Feel blessed and abundant. Feel good. This will send a signal to the Universe and more good will come to you. The opposite is also true.

The right way of practicing Creative Visualization is the one in which the one who visualizes accepts, believes, and has no doubts about the vision coming true. Actually, he feels that what he desires is already a reality and that it is just a matter of time and space for him to experience it. He believes that it's done already.

Well, through the practice of meditation and mindful living you climbed up to those higher levels of existence from where you see interminable possibilities and feel your connection with a source of unending and enormous power. Now that you see potential in you and possibilities all around you... now that you see the Divine Intelligence manifesting all around you... now that you see magic and miracles all around you... now that you realize that you too are a miracle, a magic occurrence, a manifestation of Love… you are ready to believe.

Believing is so important.

Believe!

Believe and you will receive!

Believe that it is just a matter of time for your dreams to come true. Believe in a relaxed way, that everything has already happened. No big deal! Consider it done. It is just a matter of time for you to see it. It's coming your way.

We will be talking about positive affirmation on the next chapter, but here are two affirmations that I recommend you to internalize:

"Everything that is good is coming my way."

"Everything that is good is here with me already. And more keeps coming my way."

Our job is to allow Love to flow freely through us. More than to create, our job is to allow our beautiful life to emerge by removing the obstacles that we ourselves have put there. Our job is to connect with the Source and allow the Life Force to flow freely through us. Our job is to allow the Holy Spirit to operate in us and through us so we may be able to give our unique contributions to the world. This does not demand hard work. All it demands is for us to get out of the way.

Mind shapes reality. Set your sight on the goals. Focus on the results. Create a picture, a movie in your mind where you see yourself doing what you like and living the life of your dreams. Watch this movie all the time. Feel how good you feel. Create a real picture. Draw it, paint it, or put together a collage. Look at it everyday. Believe it! See it! Feel it! And take action!

You may not know how your dream will come true, but don't worry about that. As Earl Nightingale once said, *"All you have to do is know where you're going. The answers will come to you of their own accord."* Don't obsess with the "how." Set your eyes on the goal and believe that the Universe will take care of the details. Do not fall into the trap of waiting until conditions are right to take action. Keep your eyes on the goal and take action now.

Here are five steps that can help you in the process of visualization:

1 – Express gratitude
2 – Ask what you want
3 – Visualize vividly
4 - Believe you have already received
5 – Express gratitude again

Let's review them one by one.

1 – Express gratitude

Think of all the things, people and situations that you are grateful for now. Give thanks. Think of all the things, people and situations of your past. Give thanks. Make it your habit to express gratitude many times a day. Say "Thank you" all the time. Give thanks all the time. Live in a state of thanksgiving.

2 – Ask what you want

Decide what you want. Let the Universe know what you want. Place the order. Write it down in the present tense, as if you had already received whatever you have asked for and are giving thanks for it. "I am so happy for now I have…"

3 – Visualize vividly

Imagine it. Dream it. Create clear pictures -- imaginary or real – and see you living the life you want. Keep these images alive in you all the time.

4 – Believe you have already received

Imagine, visualize and believe that you can have what you want. Believe that you deserve what you want. Believe that what you want is a real possibility for you. Believe that what you asked for is already yours. Feel the feelings of already having it. Live as if you already had it. Give thanks for it.

5 – Express gratitude again

Imagine how you are going to feel when your wishes come to be, and feel that way now. Feel good. Feel happy. Feel high, exhilarated, overjoyed, ecstatic! Feel blessed. Feel grateful. Now! Give thanks. Now! Give thanks for the gifts that have not yet arrived but that are coming your way. Now!

Throughout this process remember that feelings are of the utmost importance. Allow yourself to feel your desires in your bones. Yearn for them. Allow yourself to feel your desires fulfilled. See yourself possessing what you want. And feel the feelings you will feel when your desires are fulfilled.

Now that we have understood the power of visions, let us explore the power of words. In our next chapter we will learn how to incorporate positive affirmations in what we are doing in order to manifest the lives of our dreams.

Piero Falci

CHAPTER SEVEN

POSITIVE AFFIRMATIONS

"In the beginning was the Word, and the Word was with God, and the Word was God." – John 1:1

We have just learned about the power of images. Now we will reflect on the power of words. We've seen that our dreams shape our reality, and the same is true about our self-talk. We talk to ourselves all the time, but are we aware of what we are telling ourselves? Is it positive?

Do you remember that when we discussed meditation and mindfulness we learned that we can scan our thoughts and emotions, that we can identify those thoughts that bring negative emotions to the surface, and that we can take corrective measures? Well, we can also identify the negative conversations taking place in our heads and put optimism and confidence in their place. We can let the negative self-talk go and replace it with positive affirmations.

Now this is fun! You can create your life by choosing what you tell yourself. Your self-talk determines your life. Positive thoughts, positive visions, positive self-talk, positive speech, and positive actions together bring about awesome lives!

Create your own positive affirmations. Write them down and read them daily, in the mornings and in the evenings. Create a poem with them and recite it many times a day. Write a song and sing it. Record your affirmations, the poem, and the song with your own voice, and listen to them regularly. Let them become the soundtrack of your life. Experience the power of listening to yourself describing your dreams. There are many ways of making it easy for you to go back to your life goals and affirmations on a regular basis. See what works for you. Ideas? Use the voice recorder on your phone to record your voice. Use a camera to record yourself talking about your ideal life.

When we affirm we re-program our self-talk. Words are powerful, so we should use them carefully because we manifest what we say. As Don Miguel Ruiz reminds us, we must be impeccable with our words.

THE CLEARING TECHNIQUE

Whenever you write a goal, you may be haunted by doubts. The Clearing Technique -- presented by Shakti Gawain on the "Creative Visualization Workbook. Use the Power of Your Imagination to Create What You Want in Your Life" -- is a simple practice to help you clear doubts that you will be able to achieve what you want.

Here's how you do it…

Write your goal and then write down all the reasons that come to your mind -- every doubt, every objection, every fear, everything -- that makes you think that you can't have what you want. Come back to your list until you feel you have listed everything. Now look at your list and write a positive affirmation to counteract each objection. Focus on the most powerful affirmations and meditate on them every day along with your original goal. Examples: "My higher self is guiding me to my perfect body. I deserve to be healthy and beautiful. My higher self is guiding me to be successful. I deserve to do what I do best, and make lots of money doing it."

CHAPTER EIGHT

THE JFT TECHNIQUE

You are, now, well equipped to take action every single day to remove the self-imposed obstacles and allow the Life Force to flow freely through you, knowing that this is what will bring about what you want in your life.

Since goal-setting is just the beginning of the process, you will now learn how to revisit your goals and practice the techniques you have learned with regularity.

The Just For Today technique is based on something very simple: making and keeping promises.

You will select a large goal, break it down into smaller goals, and then you will make a promise introducing the "Just For Today" preamble. Here's an example:

Imagine that you want to be healthier, and that your doctor told you that you have to reduce the amount of sugar in your diet. Imagine that you love sweets and that you have developed the habit of eating chocolate everyday, many times a day. How do you apply the JFT technique? Well, in this case you could promise yourself the following: "Just for today, when the desires to eat chocolate kick in, at least once, I will not give in. Just for today, at least one time during the day, I will decide not to eat chocolate when the desire pops up."

So let us go through this in more detail:

The craving to eat chocolate kicks in. How do you react? What feelings pop up? Are you able to pause and take some time to think about what you are going to do? Let's imagine that you cannot control the craving. How do you feel? Do you feel guilty? Do you feel that you are a lost case? Do you feel powerless? Worthless?

OK, that's the scenario. Let me give you a map that will take you through a new road that will lead you to the desired destination. This map is based on the method that you have learned and are now practicing.

<><><>

To make it easier for you to understand, I will explain the application of the JFT technique twice. Let's take a first look:

<><><>

Using the example above, what should you do when the craving to eat chocolate kicks in?

1 – Pause. You have received a stimulus. Don't react thoughtlessly. Take control of your response. Widen the space between the stimulus and the response. Remember this quote: *"Between stimulus and response there is a space. In that space is our power to choose our response. In our response lies our growth and our freedom."* ~ Viktor E. Frankl. Don't you want to grow? Don't you want to be free? Don't you want to live the life of your dreams? So, pause, widen the gap, and choose your best response.

2 – Begin with the commitment that you will always be gentle with yourself. Do not entertain negative feelings toward yourself. Do the opposite and praise yourself for the progress you are making.

3 - Express gratitude for your body. "I am grateful for my body. I am grateful for everything my wonderful body allows me to do. I am in awe with my body and with the intelligence that governs it and keeps life going."

4 - Renew your commitment to not worry, to not be afraid.

5 - Renew your commitment to not get angry. Do not get angry with yourself or anyone else.

6 - Renew your commitment to be honest and keep your promises. Be authentic and honest.

7 - Visualize yourself in a perfect body. Know that you already are in the shape you desire. Feel it.

8 - Affirm. "I am on my way of allowing my perfect body to come to light. My perfect body is already here. I am on a journey of allowing it to reveal itself to the world. I am removing the obstacles and allowing the Divine Intelligence to heal and reveal my magnificent body."

9 – Apply the JFT technique. "Just for today, I will reduce the intake of chocolate. I can do this easily. Just for today, I will pause and allow the Divine Force to support me in making the right decisions. Just for today, I am perfectly capable of doing it."

Apply all techniques to help you move forward with your goal of being healthier. Visualize yourself in a healthy, vibrant body. Visualize yourself not craving chocolate any longer. Visualize yourself disliking the taste of chocolate. Create positive affirmations that emphasize that having a healthy body and eating a healthy diet come naturally and easily for you.

But, again, the key is to make and keep those little promises. It can be really easy. Break big projects into manageable parts. Break big life-changing goals into smaller, achievable, daily goals. Make and keep those little promises. Here are other examples:

- I love my body. I love myself. Just for today, when I feel like smoking, I will stop and decide not to, and I will do this at least once during the day. I can easily skip lighting up one cigarette. I see myself healthier and in excellent shape.
- I love my body. I love myself. Just for today when the thought that I don't have time to exercise emerges, I will not give in. I will exercise, even if it is doing just few repetitions of one single exercise for one minute. I see myself healthier and in better shape.

<><><>

Now, let us take a second look at the application of the JFT technique.

<><><>

The JFT technique helps us bring together all we have been talking about in the previous chapters. In order to apply the technique let's begin by finding a quiet and comfortable place. Find the time to do this everyday. Choose a time and location that allow you to relax and focus on this exercise without interruption. You will relax your body and mind using the techniques you learned in the meditation chapter of this book.

Let's use an example: You want to have a healthier body free of pain and illness.

What should you do?

You should affirm, visualize and feel, focusing on the 5 following areas that are inspired by the 5 Reiki precepts:
   1. Gratitude
   2. Fearlessness
   3. Patience and Forgiveness
   4. Honesty
   5. Love and Kindness

1 – Gratitude: Just for Today I will be grateful

- Affirm: I am grateful for my body and everything it does for me and has done for me all my life. My body has allowed me to enjoy my life and the world around me.

- Visualize: See all the wonderful things you are able to do because of your body. You can enjoy food. You can take a walk on the beach. You can hold and smell a flower. You can laugh. You can speak. You can hug a loved one. You can hold a baby. You can see a beautiful sunrise. You can listen to birds singing or the wind moving the branches of trees.

- Feel the gratitude in your heart. Allow the gratitude to move through your body. Imagine it is a light the fills your whole body. Feel it filling you completely and over-pouring the limits of your physical body and just pouring out into the world until it fills everything around you. Feel it in your bones. Feel how grateful you are for your healthy body and all it can do. Imagine how it feels and allow the feeling to fill your whole body.

2 – Fearlessness: Just for Today I will not worry

- Affirm: I let go of all worry. I am fearless and bold. I trust in the wisdom of my body to heal itself. I trust in my ability to accomplish my goals. I trust in the willingness of Universe to help me have a healthy body.

- Visualize: See all the wonderful things your body can do when it is healthy. See yourself running, climbing, dancing and a whole variety of activities you enjoy when your body is healthy. See yourself buying new clothes to fit into this new healthy body.

- Feel: Allow yourself to have the feelings you would have while doing these activities. Imagine how it feels to run on the beach, or walking, or dancing, or doing any other activity in your healthier body. Imagine how it feels and allow the feeling to fill your whole body.

3 - Patience and Forgiveness: Just for Today I will not anger

- Affirm: I let go of anger. I am patient and accepting of my body and myself. I forgive myself and let go of blame and guilt. I am innocent. I am good. I am a perfect child of the universe. I am free to make good choices for myself today.

- Visualize: See yourself making the choices that serve your highest good. See yourself forgiving anyone that you are harboring any ill feeling for as it relates to your health. If there are persons in your life that you have been blaming, see yourself forgiving them the same way you have forgiven yourself. Hug them. Say kind words to them. Set them free of blame or guilt.

- Feel this beautiful tenderness as you understand that you are innocent and that all the others in your life that you thought were guilty of anything are innocent too. Feel the peace that fills your heart and your whole being as you forgive and free yourself and others of any blame. Imagine how it feels and allow the feeling to fill your whole body.

4 – Honesty: Just for Today I will be honest

- Affirm: I am transparent with myself and others. I accept responsibility for my choices. I accept myself and do not try to be someone else. I do not make excuses for myself or others. I am true to myself. I am willing to do the work required to reach my goals.

- Visualize: I see myself working towards my goal. I see myself exercising. I see myself eating the right food. I see myself living stress free and enjoying my work and my life.

- Feel: I feel the relaxation in my body. I feel the freedom of not needing to pretend that I am someone else. I am free and feel this freedom in my entire being. Every cell in my body is able to function effortlessly because my whole being is relaxed in the knowledge that I do not have to pretend anymore and that I am being my authentic self. Imagine how it feels and allow the feeling to fill your whole body.

5 - Love and Kindness: Just for Today I will be loving and kind

- Affirm: I am gentle with myself and others. I accept myself and take care of myself. I allow myself to flow in harmony with the Universe. I let go of resistance or struggle. I accept myself. I accept others. I let go of expectations and judgment. I respect myself and I respect others. I treat my body with reverence, love and respect.

- Visualize: I see myself interacting harmoniously with myself and others. I see myself taking care of me. I see myself honoring my desires and needs. I see myself honoring the desires and needs of others. I see myself taking care of my body: eating the right food, exercising and keeping myself stress free.

- Feel: I feel the love of the universe pouring through me and healing my body. I feel every cell of my body full of the Love Energy of the Universe. Light is filling me. Love is filling and guiding me. I feel my connection to the Universal Love and through this connection my body becomes healthy. Imagine how it feels and allow the feeling to fill your whole body.

So now you know the formula. It's quite simple, isn't it? Cultivate gratitude, fearlessness, patience and forgiveness, honesty, loving kindness while affirming, visualizing and feeling.

It has been said that it takes 21 days to develop a habit. I challenge you to practice the techniques contained in this book for 21 days without interruption. In case you skip one day, I challenge you to start all over again. Go back and consider the day you come back as the first one of the 21 days. Practice the method for 21 days. Record your progress on a journal. And begin to see your wishes coming true!

Populate your day with those JFT commitments that will help you create healthy habits:

- Just for today I will meditate.
- Just for today I will let go of things that hold me back.
- Just for today I will live mindfully.
- Just for today I will scan my thoughts and emotions.
- Just for today I will revisit my goals twice a day.
- Just for today I will visualize.
- Just for today I will practice positive affirmations.
- Just for today I will practice the JFT technique.

CHAPTER NINE

THE PEACEFUL WAYS METHOD - A SUMMARY

Congratulations!

You have reached the end of the first part of this book and by now you know how the process of manifesting your wishes works. This is just a quick review to remind you of what to do.

In order to manifest my dreams:

1. I will exercise my birthright and gently give myself time to rest. I will choose to be gentle with myself always. I will, through meditation, go to the center of my being and get in touch with the Mighty Force everyday. Aware of that Higher Energy that is everywhere and creates everything, I will tenderly remove the obstacles that prevent its free flow through me, knowing that once I allow it to flow freely through me, once I allow who I really am to come to light, all my wishes will come true.

2. I will identify all those things I should be grateful for, and express my gratitude. I will affirm my commitment to not allow worries, doubts and fears to trouble me. I will let go of worries and ill-feelings toward myself and others.

3. I will reflect on who I am and why I am here. In the silent chamber of my heart, I will listen. I will accept my Call to Adventure. I will set goals that are in accordance with who I am and my purpose to be here. I will be authentic and honest with myself and others.

4. I will be loving and kind with myself and others.

5. I will practice Creative Visualization.

6. I will practice Positive Affirmations.

7. I will practice the JFT technique.

And by doing all this, all my wishes will come true.

PART II

PART II

Part I of the book presents the Peaceful Ways Method of making wishes come true. It contains everything you need to know to get yourself in motion. Follow those instructions and you will make your wishes come true.

Part II presents additional material that you may find useful to support you on your journey. It contains reflections on the techniques, as well as insights that came up during my meditations.

As I said, you may find the ideas contained in Part II useful, but you can skip them completely and concentrate on practicing what is presented on Part I of the book, since that is what will help you bring about the life of your dreams.

CHAPTER TEN

EBB AND FLOW
AND
MIND CONTROL

Sometimes we feel like superheroes, ready to face life's greatest challenges. Other times we feel like timid cowards, wanting to flee and hide. Sometimes we feel courageous, optimistic, determined and confident, while other times we experience fear, pessimism, hesitation, and doubt. One day we wake up full of positive energy, but many are the days when we feel so depleted that even getting out of bed is difficult.

Have you ever asked yourself, "Why?"

Why do we go through these mood fluctuations? What is it that hurls us to the highest peaks one day and pulls us down to the lowest valleys the next? And is there a way to avoid the descent into the doldrums?

James Allen, the author of "As A Man Thinketh," clearly made the point: we are what we think! Since the quality of our lives is determined by the quality of our thoughts, we better make sure we select our thoughts wisely.

The key that opens the door to the kingdom of serenity is the understanding that our thoughts influence our moods, and if we want to live a happy, productive life we should learn to scan and select our thoughts.

The prescription may sound simple, but if we practice it with diligence, eventually we will be able to tame melancholy and gloom.

So, here's my recommendation:

1 – Meditate everyday. Separate yourself from your thoughts. You are not your thoughts. You are the one who observes them.

2 – Bring what you have learned during the meditation practice to your day and scan your thoughts and feelings. Be the one who observes your moods. Be aware of your feelings. Ask yourself, "What am I feeling? Why am I feeling this way? Why am I fearful? Why am I enraged? Why am I sad?" Be the one who identifies the thoughts behind the moods. Screen your thoughts many times during the day. "What am I thinking? How are my thoughts affecting my mood?" Remember that you are not your moods either; you are the one who observes them and is capable of choosing which ones should stay and which ones should go.

3 – Spot the ugly ego at work, ready to get a hold of you and bring you down. Be the one who observes the ego, and when a dangerous situation arises, be ready to say, "There you are, hiding in the bushes. I see you. I'm not going to stay here and play your game. I am moving on to a better place. Good-bye."

4 – Put a positive spin on your thinking. Learn techniques that allow you to shift from negative to positive self-talk. Practice the techniques of creative visualization and positive affirmations. The moment you identify a negative thought in your mind, gently let it go, and replace it with the best positive image of yourself surrounded by affirmations such as, "I am prospering everyday. I am growing in health, love, wealth and wisdom everyday. I am advancing and moving forward everyday. All that is good is coming my way."

5 – Finally, do what makes you feel good. Surround yourself with positive, supportive, happy people. Smile a lot and laugh more. Adopt a healthy lifestyle, a healthy diet, and learn techniques to manage stress.

The practice of meditation helps immensely with these aforementioned points. When we meditate, we learn to observe our thoughts: we acknowledge the thoughts, and gently release them, without initiating an inner narrative or dialogue. The greatest benefit of meditation is equipping us to screen our moods, our thoughts, and our egos at work during the other hours of the day when we are not meditating. It is through the practice of meditation that we realize that we are not our moods, our thoughts and our egos; we are separated from them. We are the ones who observe them. Through practice, we learn not to engage with negative thoughts; we learn to let them simply pass.

The practice of creative visualization and positive affirmations helps us reduce the negative self-talk. Soon, we will find ourselves criticizing less, looking for the good in every situation, and expressing gratitude more often. It may take some time, but this practice produces optimists. You have everything you need to become one. Remember: "As a man thinks in his heart, so is he."

Do these things and not only you will be blessed but you will also be a blessing to the world.

Piero Falci

CHAPTER ELEVEN

POSITIVE THOUGHTS AND FEEL-GOOD FEELINGS

The secret to a good life is to populate your mind and heart with positive thoughts and feel-good moments, giving no room for negativity.

Whenever you fear that something bad may happen, or that you may not have enough, the best thing you can do is to immediately acknowledge that you are having negative thoughts. Remember that you are not your thoughts; you are the one having the thoughts. Notice that you have noticed that you are having the thoughts, therefore you are separated from your thoughts, and you can choose not to stay with them.

Every time you become aware that you are being attacked by negative thoughts and feelings — such as fears, doubts, and worries of any nature – stop and say to yourself, "Here they are again. I know where these negative thoughts will take me if I let them; they will take me to the emotional doldrums. I choose not to go there, and I am not going there. I choose not to give space to fear, worry and anxiety."

<><><>

A friend of mine developed his own technique to deal with negative thoughts: he imagines that he is watching the thoughts on the screen of an imaginary TV. Once he notices that he is being sucked into a melodrama and negative emotions that are not doing him any good, he simply turns the imaginary TV off. That's all. Negative thoughts and emotions are gone. This works for him, and you can develop your own way of sending negative thoughts away.

What do we need to do to populate our minds with positive thoughts?

1 - Begin by giving thanks for all the good you have already received and for all the good that you will soon receive.

2 - Quietly go to the sacred center of your being, and restore your confidence in the abundance of the Universe. Mentally, imagine yourself going with confidence to the inexhaustible source of all that is good in the Universe, and feel yourself receiving much more than what you need or ask for. You will always have everything you need and desire. It is your birthright.

3 - Experience the feeling that you are divinely protected and abundantly blessed. Peace, harmony, success, achievement, well-being, and perfect health are yours. In your mind, see images of yourself experiencing abundance. In your body, feel the tranquility of having a healthy body. Feel the serenity that comes with knowing that you have and will always have everything you need. Feel the joy of living a life blessed with an abundance of good things.

4 - Every time any worry about the future emerges, replace the negative with positive. Practice positive self-talk. Give thanks. Gently bring to your mind positive affirmations.

Do this over and over again throughout your days, no matter how many times it may be necessary, no matter how many times negative thoughts come to haunt you. As you continue to do this diligently, the negative thoughts will dwindle away and more good things will come your way.

This – what I have just described above -- is prayer.

Believe, and you will receive!

Practice, practice, practice, over and over again, and you will certainly experience all the good things that have always been and will always be available to you.

Namaste!

The Divine in me recognizes the Divine all around me, gives thanks and rejoices.

Namaste!

Piero Falci

CHAPTER TWELVE

GOOD IS COMING MY WAY

Begin by examining your desires.

Make sure that what you want is what you really want, not what the world told you to want.

Be authentic.

Make sure that your desires are in alignment with your highest purpose in life.

Once you have clear that what you desire is actually what is best for you and for the highest good of all, focus your thoughts on imagining your desires fulfilled, and try to feel now the same joy you will feel when your dreams come true.

Here's a positive affirmation that you can use:

"Everything that is good is coming my way. Everything that does not serve the Highest Good is going away. All that is good comes my way and stays with me. Everything that does not serve the Highest Good has moved away from me and will never come back."

Just say it, in front of a mirror if possible.

Open your arms and while you say, "Everything that is good is coming my way," bring your hands toward your chest, palms facing in.

Feel everything that is good coming to you, and embrace the good feelings.

Once your hands are near your body, gently rotate them, and with the palms of your hands now facing outward, say, "Everything that does not serve the Highest Good is going away."

Say these words while imagining that you are gently and successfully pushing every obstacle away from you with your hands.

Repeat at least three times, and every time, open a wider smile.

<><><>

Feel free to create your own affirmations. Here are some suggestions:

"Everything that is good is coming my way."

"Everything that is good is here with me already. And more keeps coming my way."

"Everything that is good comes to me and stays with me."

"Everything that does not serve the Highest Good has moved away from me and will never come back."

<><><>

CHAPTER THIRTEEN

PROMISES AND POSITIVE SELF-TALK

The Optimist Creed

Promise yourself

To be so strong that nothing can disturb your peace of mind

To talk health, happiness, and prosperity to every person you meet

To make all your friends feel that there is something worthwhile in them

To look at the sunny side of everything and make your optimism come true

To think only of the best, to work only for the best and to expect only the best

To be just as enthusiastic about the success of others as you are about your own

To forget the mistakes of the past and press on to the greater achievements of the future

To wear a cheerful expression at all times and give a smile to every living creature you meet

To give so much time to improving yourself that you have no time to criticize others

To be too large for worry, too noble for anger, too strong for fear, and too happy to permit the presence of trouble

To think well of yourself and to proclaim this fact to the world, not in loud word, but in great deeds

To live in the faith that the whole world is on your side, so long as you are true to the best that is in you

~ Christian D. Larson

The secret to improving our lives is to make promises and keep them. The Optimist Creed is an example of a series of superior promises that if kept will surely enhance anyone's life. So here's one thing you can do to develop your positive self-talk: memorize The Optimist Creed and recite it everyday.

Want to do something even better? Re-write the creed using "I." Example: "I promise myself to be so strong that nothing can disturb my peace of mind." Go ahead and do it. Memorize it. Recite it. Practice, practice, practice, over and over again, and you will certainly experience all the good things that have always been and will always be available to you.

Namaste!

The Divine in me recognizes the Divine everywhere, all around me, gives thanks, and rejoices.

Namaste!

CHAPTER FOURTEEN

DOUBLE H, DOUBLE W

Paula and I came up with the "Double H Double W Salutation." When we see each other we signal two fingers up twice, followed by three fingers up, also twice. The two fingers remind us of the letter H and the three fingers of the letter W.

Double H for Happy and Healthy. Double W for Wealthy and Wise. The gesture reminds us that "I am Happy. I am Healthy. I am Wealthy. I am Wise."

A good friend told me that this brought back memories of her childhood. She told me that one of the preferred sayings of her father was, "Early to bed, and early to rise, makes a man Healthy, Wealthy and Wise." I will add the word "Happy" to that saying. "Early to bed, and early to rise, makes a man Happy, Healthy, Wealthy and Wise."

Everyday, during my daily practice of meditation, visualization, I recite the following positive affirmations:

The universal, intelligent, loving and healing Energy flows freely through me.

It purifies me.

It heals me.

It protects me.

I am healed physically, mentally, emotionally and spiritually.

My body is healthy.

My mind is clear.

My heart is joyful.

My soul is serene.

I am happy.

I am healthy.

I am wealthy.

I am wise.

<><><>

Go forth and make this day a great day! And why stop there? Do more than that. Be bold. Go forth and make this day The Best Day Ever!

Namaste!

CHAPTER FIFTEEN

AFFIRMING A JOYFUL LIFE

Here are some positive affirmations. You can read them all at once, or you can choose just one and cherish it throughout your day. Simply feel what is best for you.

I am prospering everyday. I feel it.

I am growing in health, love, happiness, wealth, serenity, and wisdom everyday. I feel it.

I am getting healthier everyday. I feel it.

The love I give and receive expands everyday. I feel it.

The good I seek is seeking me. I feel it.

My wealth is multiplying everyday. I feel it.

I experience more serenity and peace everyday. I feel it.

My consciousness expands everyday. I feel it.

I am getting wiser everyday. I feel it.

I grow in gratitude everyday. I feel it.

I am advancing and moving forward in all aspects of my life everyday. I feel it.

My life is good and is getting better everyday. I feel it.

I am connected to the inexhaustible and generous Source of All that keeps providing abundantly everyday. I feel it.

More and more good things keep coming to me everyday. I feel it.

Everything that is good is coming my way. Everything that does not serve the Highest Good is moving away.

<><><>

If you want to be inspired by the power of Positive Affirmations, I recommend you get a copy of Louise Hay's "You Can Heal Your Life." It is a wonderful book who has helped millions around the world. Here's one of Louise's powerful affirmations:

In the infinity of life where I am,
all is perfect, whole and complete.
Each one of us, myself included, experiences the richness
and fullness of life in ways that are meaningful to us.
I now look at the past with love and choose
to learn from my old experiences.
There is no right or wrong, nor good or bad.
The past is over and done.
There is only the experience of the moment.
I love myself for bringing myself
through this past into this present moment.
I share what and who I am,
For I know we are all one in Spirit.
All is well in my world.
~ Louise Hay

CHAPTER SIXTEEN

JUST FOR TODAY
I WILL BE GRATEFUL

"Just for today, I will be grateful." This is the first of five Reiki precepts.

Pause for an instant and ask yourself, "To be grateful... to live with the attitude of gratitude... What exactly does that mean? What does it demand from me? How does a person who is full of gratitude live?"

Here are four ideas you may want to incorporate in your days:

1 – Just for today, I will pay attention to everything and everyone, and acknowledge the many things I should be thankful for.

2 – Just for today, I will live expressing gratitude for as many things as possible, as many times as possible.

3 – Just for today, I will be grateful not only for what I already have but for all the many blessings that are coming my way.

4 – Just for today, I will not want.

This last one seems to oppose what this book is about. Isn't this book about helping me make my dreams come true? Am I not being guided to express my desires and manifest them? How come, then, I am being directed to "not want?" Well, think about it: in order to live in a state of blissful gratitude, we have to manage our desires. We cannot let them run amok. If we keep wanting all the time, there's no room for thankfulness. So, curbing our desires is also a healthy practice.

PRAYER OF ACCEPTANCE AND GRATITUDE

Today, I will not want anything. I will not want to be different. I will not want to be who I am not. I will accept myself just as I am.

Today, I will bask in the realization that I am a manifestation of the Eternal Life Energy. I will feel how unique, wonderful, and magnificent I am.

Today, I will relax and accept myself completely. I will feel that I don't have to do anything because I already am whole, perfect and complete.

Today, I will feel that I don't have to get anywhere else because where I am, wherever it may be, is my home.

Today, I will not want my life to be different, I will not want my situation to be different, I will not want my day to be different, I will not want others to be different.

Today, I will accept whatever and whoever comes to me as a gift that I should pay attention to and be grateful for. I will feel that everything is perfect just as it is.

Today I will feel happy, content and satisfied.

HAPPINESS THROUGH GRATEFULNESS

Why practicing gratitude is so important? Because gratitude is the key that opens the door to the Kingdom of Happiness.

I am grateful for having reached the knowing that I have control over my moods and that I can be happy if I so choose. I am grateful for knowing the things that make me happy. I am grateful that I can do the things that make me happy. I am grateful for being happy. And I have realized that the main practice that brings me happiness is gratefulness.

Do you want to be happy?

OK, here's the formula, and it's quite simple.

There are three things that you should do to achieve happiness:

First, be grateful.

Second, be grateful.

Third, be grateful.

By doing so, suddenly, you will experience happiness. And then, you will realize how grateful you are for being this happy person. And then, you will realize that you are happy because you practice gratitude.

It is by practicing gratefulness that we achieve happiness. Or, as Brother David Steindl-Rast puts it, *"In daily life we must see that it is not happiness that makes us grateful, but gratefulness that makes us happy."*

So, if you want to be happy, the first thing you have to do is to give thanks, the second thing is to give thanks, and the third thing is to give thanks.

Try it. You'll be amazed how well it works!

Gratitude is the practice that enhances lives, produces happiness, and betters the world.

THINGS TO BE GRATEFUL FOR

Here's a life-changing exercise. Write down every day three things that you are grateful for. Here are some examples:

1 – I am grateful for my life, this wonderful opportunity to learn, grow, and develop. Thank you, Forces of the Universe, my Mother and my Father, who brought me here.

2 – I am grateful for being able to meditate, and I am thankful to all the many masters who have taught me how to meditate and keep reminding me to meditate.

3 – I am thankful for my family, my loved ones, the ones I love the most, such great companions on this mysterious journey. Thank you for being in my life, and allowing me to experience love to a degree that I never experienced before.

4- I am thankful for my friends, gifts that God gave me. They are my companions and they support me on the journey of learning and growth. How blessed I am for having them in my life!

5 – I am thankful for those moments when I have no worries, and I experience the peaceful confidence that everything is unfolding exactly as it should, that everything is and will be alright, and that there is nothing to be afraid of.

6 – I am thankful for the Forces of the Universe that move me to take action and do what I can, within my possibilities and according to my talents and skills, to make this world a better place. I feel that I am giving my contribution, and that is a very comforting feeling.

7 – I am grateful for the authors who share their wisdom with me, and teach me how to live a better life.

8 – I am thankful for being able to reflect and put my fears in perspective. Everything is OK and will be OK. Life is unfolding as it should. I am where I am for a reason. There are lessons to be learned and contributions to be given. Everyday I remember the Reiki precept, "Just for today I will not worry." What am I afraid of? There's compassion, love, and generosity in all of us. Once and for all: there's nothing to be afraid of. I am grateful for the message, "Be not afraid."

9 – I am grateful for my house, my garden, my shower, the water that comes out of the faucet, my appliances, and the food in my refrigerator and pantry. Thank you, all of you, who I don't personally know. Thank you for making available to me all the things that make my life so much more comfortable. Thank you.

Piero Falci

CHAPTER SEVENTEEN

JUST FOR TODAY
I WILL NOT WORRY

"Just for today, I will not worry." This is the second of five Reiki precepts.

Pause for an instant and ask yourself, "How can someone not worry? Is it possible to live without worries?"

Let us begin this exploration reflecting on what worries are and where they come from. Worries are those disturbing thoughts that bring about distressful emotions such as fear, apprehension, anxiety, anguish, and tension. They are generated by excessive and sometimes obsessive thinking about misfortune and danger, either real or imaginary.

Many times, negative emotions emerge from revisiting situations, and other times we worry too much about the future. We have to pause and ask ourselves, "What am I worrying about right now? Why do I worry? Is my reason for worrying a valid one?" Many times, there are no well-founded reasons for worrying, but we keep doing it just because we have developed a bad habit. The truth is that worrying doesn't do us any good; it just makes us feel worse and consumes our energy. Worrying doesn't change anything; only action does.

My friend Bob, who has faced very tough times in his life, tells me, "You know what I do? I pause and ask myself, 'What is the worst that can happen?' Then I look back, at what I went through, and I realize that I will be able to handle even that. I know that I am able to handle anything. Therefore, I don't worry."

The truth is that worry is useless.

Why worry about things we have no control over? If we don't have control, our worry will not change the outcome a bit. And why worry about the things we can control? If we do have control, then we can take action and influence the outcome. So, the reality is that we should never worry. We should not worry about the things we cannot control, and we should not worry about the things we can control.

As the Dalai Lama said, *"If it can be solved, there's no need to worry. And if it can't be solved, worry is of no use."* In my own words, "If you have control, don't worry. And, if can't control, why worry?"

SCANNING THOUGHTS

In our conversations, my father almost invariably reminds me to embrace and practice Positive Thinking. He always finds a way of including the recommendation, "Pensamento Positivo!" during our exchanges.

He is right: thoughts are powerful. We must practice to imagine only the best outcomes.

These days, when I catch myself having negative thoughts, I tell myself, "Delete." This is a reminder to pause, acknowledge that the thoughts I am having are not good for me. It works as a command to get rid of negative thoughts, and replace them with positive ones. I tell myself, "Delete! Positive Thinking!" And this simple technique works for me.

LIVING MINDFULLY

One way of worrying less is to focus on the here-now by practicing mindful living.

So, pay attention and be alert. Stay in the here-now as much as possible, but do not use the here-now as an escape from facing your problems. Deal with your problems, past and present ones, and prepare yourself for the future. Adequate planning is always healthy. Plan your work, and work your plan everyday. Do something, no matter how little, to better your life and achieve your dreams. Make promises and keep them; not only the promises you make to others, but especially the commitments you make to yourself. Be honest with your own self.

Again, the second precept of Reiki invites us to choose a worry-free life. How do we do it? Well, I have learned that reflecting on the Reiki precepts everyday, many times a day, and committing to put them in practice, is an effective practice to curb worries. We can live mindfully. We can meditate, visualize and affirm. These are some of the ways of removing negative thoughts and filling the mind with positive, happy dreams. And, naturally, scanning our thoughts and applying the "Delete! Positive Thinking!" technique whenever negative thoughts arise.

WORRY-FREE LIKE A LITTLE CHILD

Finally, another way of living a worry-free life is to be more like a child.

Jesus said, *"Truly I tell you, unless you change and become like little children, you will never enter the kingdom of heaven."* I believe that the main aspect that differentiates little children from adults is the fact that little children are worry-free. They do not worry about the future. They do not spend any time imagining that bad things may happen. They are not afraid. Worry and fear are not part of their lives. They are immersed in the here-now, exercising their innate curiosity, discovering the world around them, and filling their lives with moments of awe while savoring the beauty, mystery, and wonder that surrounds them. Simply, little children are having a joyous worry-free time.

A WORRY-FREE LIFE

So here is a reflection on "Just for today, I will be free from worry…"

Just for today, I will be like a little child. I will not be afraid of anything. I will not worry about the past, present, or future. I will not fear danger or misfortune. I will not allow worry to grow within me. I will not succumb to fear. Today, I will be completely fearless. I will live this day without worrying. I will be happy. I will be curious, discover, and be amazed. I will play, have fun, smile, and have a great time.

Just for today, I will cultivate optimism. I will root out the weeds of pessimism and take good care of the plants of optimism. I will continue planting the good seeds, tending the good plants, and trusting that a plentiful harvest is coming soon to bless my honest efforts. I will keep doing the things I am being called to do trusting that every good thing is coming my way. Just for today, I will have a calm faith in a better tomorrow.

Just for today, I will use my mind to imagine, dream and visualize a happy life.

Just for today, I will not get anxious trying to do all the many things I believe I have to do in the limited time I have. I will take it easy, relax and rest. I will enjoy life. I will consider that time is an illusion, that time is on my side, and that I am ageless. I will not rush. I will not get upset if, at the end of the day, I wasn't able to do what I set myself up to do. I will realize that many of the things I thought were important, in reality were not that important, or not important at all.

If I have been able to bring joy to someone else, and make someone else's life better, I will feel happy for having had a good day.

Just for today, I will surrender to the Higher Power, and say, "Here I am. You know my intentions are pure. Help me give my gifts to the family of the Earth. Help me help others live better lives. Use me. Reward me abundantly. Give me a worry-free life!"

As Bob Marley's song goes, "Don't worry about a thing, 'cause every little thing is gonna be alright." Go forth in joy, just like a fearless, worry-free child!

I WILL NOT BE AFRAID, NO MATTER WHAT

Do you know those times when you hear things that you know you needed to hear? Well, it happened again this morning.

We were at the beach, watching the sunrise and sharing some of the lessons we've learned in life, when Nancy said something that struck me: "The time came when I decided that I would not get stressed anymore, no matter what."

I looked at her with astonishment. How can someone make such a decision? Isn't stress something beyond our control? But I instantly realized that she was dead serious. What she was saying was not some superficial nonsense, but a deep commitment, and I could tell it by the tone of her voice. She really meant it. Hers was a decision of departure without the slightest chance of return.

That was a remarkable moment for me. I immediately heard my inner voice commanding, "Pay attention, Piero. Open your ears. There is an important message here for you."

She told me that at a certain point in her life, after a series of tragic, painful events, she decided that she was not going to allow anything to stress her anymore. She had to do it, she told me, for her own sanity, to protect herself.

She, then, told me of difficult times she went through and how, by reminding herself of the promise she had made — "I will not get stressed, no matter what" — she was able, every time, to choose a better response. And what a difference this decision and practice made on the quality of her life!

I am blessed to have many awesome teachers in my life. Nancy is one of them, and she is fantastic.

She went through so much in her life! She could have chosen to be bitter, but she is one of the most positive individuals I have ever met. She always looks for the best in everything. She practices gratitude, constantly acknowledging what she has been blessed with. I admire her immensely, especially because she is this amazing human being by choice, her own. She is a living example that being in control of the quality of one's own life, by choosing the right thoughts and responses, is perfectly possible. She is a powerful role model, and she is my teacher. How fortunate I am!

So, allow me share with you the mighty lesson I learned from Nancy this morning. Maybe it can be useful to you too.

Today, I solemnly promise myself that ...

I will not get stressed, no matter what.
I will not get depressed, no matter what.
I will not be afraid, no matter what.
I will not worry, no matter what.
I will always be grateful, no matter what.

... and by remembering these promises during the tough moments, I will be able to choose the best responses, the ones that will make my life, and the lives of those around me, better.

Amen!

CHAPTER EIGHTEEN

JUST FOR TODAY
I WILL BE FREE FROM ALL ANGER

"Just for today, I will not get angry." This is the third of five Reiki Principles.

Pause for an instant and ask yourself, "What is anger? When does it come about? Why?"

Anger is an emotion that surfaces whenever someone disappoints us. We get angry at other individuals because they do not do what we want them to do, or do not behave the way we want them to behave, or do not believe in what we believe.

We also get angry whenever we disappoint ourselves.

When we regret what we have done or said, or what we have failed to say or do, we get angry.

But disproportionate auto-criticism should be avoided. We should always be gentle with ourselves, forgiving ourselves for our temporary failings and misdeeds. We should love ourselves as we are. But we also should be committed to learn from our mistakes in order not repeat them. We should love ourselves and continue the lifelong journey of bettering our own selves.

I admire all of those who make the effort to better themselves. I am thankful to them because their efforts to be better make my world better.

One of the things we should do is to observe if we are in a constant and recurring criticizing mode. If so, we should change our ways. Criticism is a big waste of time and energy. If our focus is always on what others do wrong, we become very judgmental and bitter. Spending our days criticizing others diminishes the quality of our lives.

We should resist speaking negatively about anyone. Whenever we catch ourselves about to engage in criticism, we should stop. And since the way of stopping bad behaviors is by replacing them with good ones, I submit that we should use that time to improve ourselves, in order to become the kind of individuals we respect and admire.

Make the decision that you will not allow the behavior of others to affect your moods. You will not allow them to pull your strings. You are not at their mercy. You are the captain of your own boat. You are the one pulling your own strings.

In my workshops I always ask the participants, "When was the last time you were able to change someone?" After some deliberation we all agree that we actually do not change anyone; all we can do is to inspire in others the desire to change, because change is a very personal undertaking. The best we can do is to improve our own selves, so we become examples that inspire others to do the same.

Finally, to live this precept to the fullest, one should make a commitment to not harbor any bad feelings toward anyone.

So, pause, take a deep breath, and promise yourself that...

"Just for today, I will not get angry,

I will not envy,

I will not be jealous,

I will not hate,

I will not judge,

I will not criticize,

I will not disapprove,

I will not condemn.

Just for today, I will not express any bad feelings toward anyone.

I will not hurt anyone, myself included.

I will be a loving, giving, and forgiving individual.

I will be kind, generous and patient.

I will work in becoming an improved version of myself and a blessing to the world."

Christian Larson, in his Optimist Creed, wrote, *"Promise yourself to give so much time to improving yourself that you have no time to criticize others."* Now that's a good advice, for sure! Embrace it!

Go forth in peace and joy!

Piero Falci

CHAPTER NINETEEN

JUST FOR TODAY
I WILL BE HONEST

"Just for today, I will live honestly." This is the fourth of five Reiki principles.

Honesty… we know what honesty is, right? Honest individuals are the ones who are correct and fair in all their dealings; they do not deceive, steal, cheat, mislead, exploit, or commit fraud for any reason, especially not for personal gain. They are honorable in their principles, intentions, and actions. When they profess, "I do my work honestly," they are also saying that they live honorable lives, supporting themselves and their families without harming anyone.

But besides being honest with others, there is also the commitment of honesty with oneself, which is as important as being honest with others, if not more. For me, living this commitment requires keeping the promises I make to myself, heeding my inner calling, giving expression to my life's purpose, and doing what is necessary to move my life to that place where I may be able to give my best contributions to humanity.

I am conscious that sooner or later my physical life will be over, so I am constantly asking myself, "What should I do before I die? What are the greatest contributions I can leave to the world?"

Again, I meditate on the 4 questions presented by Wayne Muller in his book, *How Then, Shall We Live? Four Simple Questions that Reveal the Beauty and Meaning of Our Lives.*

1. Who am I?

2. What do I love?

3. How do I live knowing that I will die?

4. What is my gift to the family of the Earth?

We all have unique purposes to fulfill during our lives. Our highest purposes are always calling us and seeking expression. I know that, like everybody else, I too have gifts that only I can give. My calling is to make the world better by bettering myself, and by helping other individuals better themselves. My mission is to be a guide, a helper, and a companion of other individuals on their transformational journeys, hoping that they will go through those spiritual epiphanies that will allow them to embrace a new vision for our world as a place of abundance, solidarity and peace. My highest goal is to be an agent who helps to bring Heaven to Earth. I want to spread the idea that Heaven is here, and I dream of the day when this will be the prevailing idea in mankind's collective unconscious.

So, here is my reflection on "Just for today, I will live honestly..."

Just for today, I will earn my living honestly. I will do no harm, and I will bask in the peace of mind that comes from knowing that I have been honest in all my dealings.

Just for today, I will plan my work and work my plan, because when I don't plan my work, or when I don't work as planned, not only I get disturbed, but I dishonor my highest self. So, just for today, I will pay more attention and live more mindfully. I will stay focused on my priorities and make honest choices on how to best use my time. I will reduce my exposure to distractions and be more organized, efficient, and effective. Just for today, I will execute my plans honestly.

Just for today, I will honor my parents, their parents, and all my ancestors. I will honor my teachers, their teachers, and all masters who came before me. I will honor them all by being honest and by striving to be the best that I can be.

Just for today, I will show honesty by being authentic, by being who I am meant to be, by being the best that I can be. I will be honest with myself by doing what I have been called to do. I will be honest with myself and others by living the life that only I can live, and giving the contributions that only I can give.

Just for today I will show honesty and integrity by practicing the wisdom I know manifests better lives.

<><><>

I am fully committed to be honest with myself and all other beings, and I encourage you to do the same.

Namaste!

The Divine in me recognizes the Divine in you, gives thanks, and rejoices.

Namaste!

Piero Falci

CHAPTER TWENTY

JUST FOR TODAY
I WILL BE KIND

"Do for one what you wish you could do for everyone."
~ Andy Stanley

"Just for today, I will be kind." This is the fifth of five Reiki precepts.

Kindness expresses itself in the willingness to give, to serve, to be of service. To be kind is to give… to give more than to get… to be more focused on giving and not so focused on getting… to be solely focused on giving.

Here's a suggestion. Choose one to three commitments from the list below everyday, and practice them purposefully throughout the day.

Just for today I will love, respect, and be kind with myself and all living beings.
Just for today I will show love and respect for every living thing.
Just for today I will be kind to my neighbor and all living things.

Just for today I will be generous.
Just for today I will be patient.
Just for today I will be kind.
Just for today I will be loving.
Just for today I will be giving.
Just for today I will be forgiving.
Just for today I will be compassionate.
Just for today I will be considerate.
Just for today I will be gentle.
Just for today I will be thoughtful.
Just for today I will be attentive.
Just for today I will be selfless.
Just for today I will be caring.
Just for today I will be sharing.
Just for today I will be altruistic.
Just for today I will be understanding.

Just for today I will give of myself.
Just for today I will give my time and attention to others.
Just for today I will pause and listen.
Just for today I will anticipate someone else's needs and offer help.
Just for today I will let go of my pride, and of the need to be right,
and I will forgive.
Just for today I will empathize.
Just for today I will step inside other people's shoes, understand
them, feel what they feel, feel their pain and their dreams, and help
them.

Just for today I will practice the five Reiki principles.

My life is full of gratitude, honesty and kindness, and devoid of fear
and anger.

It is a good life!

CHAPTER TWENTY ONE

MY HAPPY LIFE FORMULA

Some friends call me "Mr. Happy." Yes, like anyone else I have had many bad days in my life, full of fear, anxiety and depression, but nowadays I am in a good mood the majority of the time. I count my blessings and give thanks everyday for the life that was given to me. I smile most of the time, and I sincerely try to make others feel good. It is not uncommon for people to approach me and ask, "How come you are always so happy? What is your secret?"

I thought about the things that make me happy, and wrote them down. I created a list and called it "My Happy Life Formula." I read the list quite often to remind me of the things that make me happy. I put them in practice, and it works: they truly make me happy! I am happy because, everyday I do what I know I need to do to be happy.

1 - First and foremost, I am happy because I love myself, fully and unconditionally. I am gentle with myself. I accept myself, approve myself, and take good care of myself. There's nothing wrong with me. I am a child of God. I am whole, perfect and complete. I am.

2 - I am happy because I love my neighbors as I love myself, and because I love myself a lot, I have a lot of love to give. I sincerely

make it my objective to make other people happy. I pay attention to whoever may be in front of me at any given time, and I give them my love. This makes them happy, and it makes me happy. I am happy because I love everybody, and because everybody loves me… they may not know it yet, but eventually they will.

3 - I am happy because I know I have the power to create my own happy reality. I can select my thoughts, and replace the unattractive ones with more beautiful ones. And because I pay attention to the quality of my thoughts and do the things that make me happy, I have great, happy days, day after day, and this brings about a great, happy life.

I am happy, and the people around me are happy too. God blesses me and I am a blessing to the world. I give thanks and I am happy.

<><><>

I am convinced that happiness is independent from one's life situations and conditions. Happiness depends on a positive attitude, and it can be achieved through daily practice.

I have decided to be happy, so everyday I enhance my positive outlook by practicing what I know makes me happy.

So, here's my recipe for a happy life:
1 - Express love everyday.
2 - Appreciate what you have and give thanks everyday.
3 - See life as an adventure full of possibilities, and practice optimism everyday.
4 - Take action to improve your life everyday.
5 - Take care of your health everyday.
6 - Give of yourself everyday.

In other words, here some practical things anyone can do:
1 - Practice to express your love. Send a message to someone you love.
2 - Practice gratitude. Think of what you are grateful for.

3 - Practice optimism. List possibilities, things that would make you happy, and experience the joy of imagining them a reality.

4 - Practice to take action. Take time, everyday, to do things that you love. Also, take time, everyday, to do things that you know you should do to improve the quality of your life, even without wanting to do them.

5 - Commit to a healthy lifestyle. Remember NuRSE – Nutrition, Rest, Stretching, Exercise. If you remember this NuRSE, you may never need one.

6 - Do something to make the world better. Give some of your time, treasure, talent and touch to help others.

Remember: happiness is independent from one's life situations and conditions. Happiness depends on a positive mindset, a generous, giving heart, a commitment to take action and live a healthy lifestyle, and the daily practice of love, gratitude, and optimism.

Life is short. In order to live the best life you can live, I invite you to, everyday, make a conscious choice to be happy and do the following:

1 – Promise yourself that you will be happy. Promise that you will accept, approve and love yourself. Promise that you will always make the healthy choice. Promise that you will take good care of yourself, and put your wellbeing first. Promise that you will protect yourself and never do anything that would harm you. Promise that you will learn to love yourself and be kind to yourself, knowing that this will enhance the source of the kindness and love from where you will be able to generously give to others. Promise that you will be a blessing to the world by making others happy almost effortlessly because you are already happy. Promise that everyday you will do what you know you need to do to have a great day, and by having a series of great days you will have a great, happy life!

2 – Practice gratitude. Don't focus on what you don't have, but give thanks for what you already have.

3 – Practice mindfulness. Be here, now. Enjoy the silence. Meditate. Observe. Look at the big and the small. Be aware of the wonders surrounding you. Pay attention. Be alert. Look for beauty and goodness, and see beauty, goodness, and miracles all around you. Everything is a miracle. Every life is a miracle. Every creation is a miracle. Be conscious f the miracles. Allow yourself to be amazed. Be in connection, communication and communion with the Divine all moments of your life. Realize that this planet, all of it, wherever you may be, is holy ground. The whole Universe is our sanctuary. Live as if you are in Heaven already.

4 – Practice acceptance. It is what it is. Stop feeling frustrated, disappointed, mad and sad because the world is not the way you think it should be, or others are not the way you wanted them to be, or your life is not what you dreamt it to be. The world is the way it is, others are the way they are, and you are the way you are because we are here, all of us, to learn and to teach. You are living the experiences that you are supposed to live in order to learn the lessons you are supposed to learn, and teach the lessons you are supposed to teach. Others are also living the experiences they are supposed to live, and whatever they may be going through also creates opportunities for you to learn and to teach. So, learn and teach. Accept what is while being fully cognizant that all is changing all the time, and that you have the power to create.

5 – Be aware of change and believe in its power. Learn that you have the tremendous power to choose empowering thoughts and control your destiny. Embrace the life you already have as a point of departure to an even better life. Live the best life you can live by choosing powerful thoughts. If you don't like the life you are living, change it. Change your thoughts, and start all over again.

6 – Practice non-criticism. Break the habit of comparing yourself with others. Stop focusing on the negative aspects of someone else's life. Stop criticizing. Don't waste your time with those things. As much as possible, accept others as they are. Develop an understanding that they are on their own journeys as you are on yours. Accept the fact that everyone has his own story, and everyone

has positive and negative attributes. Focus on the positive. Look for the good in others. Look for those things in them that are worth of praise and bring a smile to your face. Be compassionate, not judgmental. If you don't have anything positive to say, don't say anything. Try to help them, but remember that you can only help those who want to be helped, and allow themselves to be helped. Try to help them but protect yourself first. Remember that your first promise is that you will choose what makes you happy and that you will protect yourself. There are things that neither you nor anyone else can do for them; they have to do on their own. There are things that they will only learn on their own time. So, develop compassion and acceptance. Love one another. Love your own self. Use your time wisely. Live your own life, not someone else's. Keep yourself so busy with your own development that you have no time to criticize others.

7 – Remember that we are one. We are all connected in ways that are beyond our understanding. What we do to others, we do to ourselves. Do good. Yes, there are bad individuals out there manipulating and exploiting others, and they seem to be getting all the good things life has to offer. Don't envy them. We reap what we sow, receive what we give, harvest what we plant. All the pain and suffering they inflict will inevitably come back to haunt them. Believe that all the good you give out will inevitably come back to bless you. Stick with the good. Do your best not to hurt anyone. Be careful about what you say and also how you say it. Mean words hurt a lot. Give of yourself to alleviate the pain and suffering of others.

8 – Don't envy. Don't be resentful or jealous that others have more than you. Believe in the abundance of the Universe and your birthright to prosper. Believe that you are a child of the Universe and that you deserve all the good the Universe has to offer. Rejoice with all that you have. Rejoice and bless others' good fortune and believe there is plenty for all.

9 – Love everybody and believe that everybody loves you. Love, care and share. Give of yourself everyday to make someone else's life a little better. Make a difference in someone else's life. Be compassionate and patient. Help others. Smile. Make them feel good

about themselves. Help the world. Do what you can to bring more justice, peace, unity and happiness to the world. Be kind, gentle and generous. Be respectful. Share your toys. And remember that it is by making others happy that you increase your own happiness.

10 – Apologize. As much as possible, repair what you may have broken. Acknowledge your errors, your faults, and don't hesitate to say, "I'm sorry." Make amends.

11 – Don't allow other people's negativity to take hold of you. Each one has his own problems. They have theirs and you have yours. Don't make someone else's problems yours. It's their problem, not yours. You already have enough problems of your own.

12 – Don't react instantly. Expand the gap between stimulus and response. Take control of your responses. Take three deep breaths before choosing your response. Even better… for no reason at all, just pause, take three deep breaths, and go back to the center of your being many times during the day.

13 – Work on completely removing complaints, regrets, and worries from your days. Don't relive the drama and the trauma. Don't store resentment. Stored resentment manifests itself as disease. Release the sad past. Stop telling your sad stories. Stop showing your wounds. Forgive everyone: others and yourself. Forgive and forget. Move on. Let go. And don't worry about the future. Worrying is nothing more than using your imagination to create something you don't want. Gently, lovingly, drop all doubts. Don't entertain negative thoughts. Fill your days with positive affirmations, and keep imagining a very successful, happy life where you are a blessing to all.

14 – Reduce the stress in your life. Stress leads to illness. Work everyday to make your life a little bit less stressful. Simplify. Don't accumulate. Get rid of the stuff you don't need. Clean up and organize your space. Fix what is broken. Do at least a little bit of what you love everyday, but also tackle some of the unpleasant but necessary tasks everyday. Plan your work and work your plan everyday.

15 – Be optimistic. Focus on what is right, good and positive, not on what is wrong, bad and negative. Choose uplifting thoughts. Say to yourself and proclaim to the world, "Life is good. Life is great. I love my life!" Cultivate hope. Believe that improvement is possible, that everything is getting better, and that the best is yet to come. Work on improving yourself, knowing that your improvement is your best contribution to the world. And remember that it doesn't matter so much what you do as the love you put into the doing. Give your contribution, however small. Plant seeds even if you are not going to be here to enjoy the fruits; someone else will. Work within your circle of influence, however small, doing the things you are able to do, however small, and then see your impact and circle of influence expand.

16 – Express love. Practice giving and receiving love. Smile. Use every opportunity you have to tell people that you love them. Look for the best in others. Make others feel good about themselves. Never underestimate the power of a good word, a compliment, a smile. Find opportunities to praise them. Let them know that you notice and appreciate who they are and the good they do. Bring a smile to their faces. Help them be the best they can be. Support their growth. Help them bring out their best and bless the world with their unique gifts. Thank them often. And whenever possible, hug them. Hugs are miraculous. Hug, don't hate.

17 – Your thoughts, words and deeds determine the quality of your life. Choose them wisely. Choose what you watch, what you read, and the people who you listen to and surround yourself with. Avoid the complainers and criticizers. Avoid the loud and aggressive ones. Choose love. Choose peace. Choose cooperation and collaboration.

18 – Your mind influences your body and your body influences your mind. Take good care of both. Practice mindfulness. Adopt a healthy lifestyle, with a good diet and physical exercise. As I say, "Choose the good NuRSE: good Nutrition, Rest, Stretching and Exercise. If you remember this NuRSE, you may never need one."

19 – Dream. Life is full of possibilities. You can do whatever you want. You can be whoever you want to be. If you are not living a life

you love, start all over again. Focus on the possibilities, and don't listen to the nay-sayers, especially the one inside your head. Imagination is a divine resource. Use it. Nurture it. Listen! What is calling you? Listen to your Highest Self and go follow your bliss.

20 – Finally, realize that everything changes. Nothing is permanent. Nothing stays the same. Don't fear death; it is inevitable. Sooner or later, it will come. Think of it as a transition, a trans-form-ation. See life as a passage, during which you were given a body. Consider that there is no beginning and no end, and that nothing is destroyed or created; it just changes form. Be courageous to resist death, but also to accept it. Live a good life so when it is all said and done you may look back and smile with no regrets. You are an eternal spiritual being having a temporary human experience. You are not your physical body. You may say that you occupy your physical body. In fact, you have occupied many physical bodies since you were born, right? Where is the newborn you once were? In the divine realm there is no death. Our Bodies change but our divine essence does not. We are changeless. We are birthless and deathless. We have died already many times during our own existence. No need to fear physical death.

There you go… my happy life formula, revised and expanded. It works for me, and I am sure it will work for you too. Apply it deliberately and diligently and enjoy an excellent, happy life!

I have decided to live, love, and be happy, deliriously happy, from this moment forward. And I am sure that the Universe shall provide. I'm playing this game. I'm in.

Blessings!

CHAPTER TWENTY TWO

ADVICE TO MY SONS

Dear sons,

There are only two lasting gifts a father can give to his children: one is roots; the other, wings. It is with a heart full of love and gratitude for all that you are, that I offer you this gift.

1 – Go do what the Forces of the Universe are calling you to do. Do not refuse the Call to Adventure. Accept it. Follow your bliss. By doing so, you will be happy. By being happy you will make others happy. And by making others happy you will be giving the greatest gift anyone can give.

2 – Dream and manifest. Learn how to dream and how to manifest your dreams. Use your imagination and take time everyday to visualize yourself living the life of your dreams. Visualize and feel how good it feels.

3 – Believe in synchronicities. Believe that as long as you are being true to yourself and following your bliss, your dreams will easily come true. You will achieve what you want with minimum effort. Helpers will show up to help you. Everything you need will reveal itself to you spontaneously, almost magically.

4 – Be authentic. Be who you are. Be who you are meant to be. Be your own unique self. That's why you are here. That's your job. That's your main job. That's your only job. That's how you bring your best contribution to the world: by being yourself... by being the best possible version of yourself. Be yourself.

5 – Don't be too harsh on yourself. Don't beat yourself down. Don't go crazy trying to be perfect, trying to be someone other than yourself; you will fail and feel inadequate. Be gentle with yourself. Love yourself. Realize that you are perfect, accomplished, and successful already. Just allow this radiant being to manifest itself. The moment you accept yourself, rejoice with your own self, and allow yourself to be who you really are, you become the gift that only you can give to the world. Just be true to yourself. Be yourself.

6 – Be in love with yourself. Be in a love affair with yourself. There's nothing selfish about it. One of the most unselfish things you can do is to love yourself, because it is by loving yourself that you will craft the best gift you can give to the world: your truest self, your best self, your magnificent presence. Love yourself. Be yourself.

7 – Don't try desperately to fit in. Don't try to please others all the time. Don't be concerned with what others may think of you. Don't live your life trying to fulfill someone else's expectations. Don't submit yourself to other people's judgments. Don't put yourself on trial, in situations where you are constantly judging yourself and feeling that you are being judged by others. Don't allow your mood to be dictated by the opinions others may have of you, by what others say about you. You don't have to prove anything to anyone, except yourself. Remember that you are immensely valuable. Don't try to be someone else just to please others. It's impossible to be someone other than yourself. Your job is to be the grandest version of yourself. Be the grandest version of yourself. Be yourself.

8 – Be grateful and be happy. Take time everyday to recognize all the many good things that you already have. Gratitude is the key that opens the gates to the playground of happiness. Be thankful and be happy.

9 - Don't believe that you have to compete all the time. Actually, you don't have to compete. Period. You don't have to prove anything to anyone. You don't have to get where anyone else has gotten, or have what someone else has acquired. You only have to challenge yourself, go beyond your own self-imposed limitations, and be the best version of yourself. In order to do so, you don't have to do anything; you just have to be. That's all. Be yourself. Let me repeat this: you don't have to do anything; you just have to be yourself. That's all, and it is enough. Without any judgment, let yourself be who you are and who you are meant to be... totally, completely, without restricting yourself. Remove all self-imposed obstacles. Remove all doubt and fear. Remove all self-criticism. Don't be the main inhibitor of your own self. You are unique and your uniqueness is your great gift to the world. Your only job in this life is to be yourself, and to see perfection in yourself and in the entire Universe. That is all. Be yourself. Be your whole self. Be your best self.

10 - Be not afraid. Do not be afraid of anything. There aren't any reasons to be afraid. Look back and see where you are, and realize that you always have been taken good care of. You are a divine spiritual being and everything you need will always be given to you. It is your birthright. So, don't be afraid. Be grateful.

11 - Let go of the need to control every aspect of life: yours and everyone else's. Just live and let live. Trust that life is unfolding exactly as it should, guided by the Supreme Intelligence of the Universe. Let go of the need to control the outcomes. Relax, take a deep breath, and see good things happening to you and around you all the time.

12 - Stay away from rigid beliefs and ideologies. Stay away from the need to judge right from wrong, good from bad. Stay away from the need to defend your position. Remain open, but true to yourself. If necessary, speak your truth gently.

13 - Life is not made of absolutes, and there will always be many things to be considered on this journey of learning and teaching. So, accept and don't accept. Don't fight and fight. Plan and don't plan. Share and don't share. Tell your dreams, plans, and desires to some people but not to others. Listen to advice and make your own decisions. Explore alternatives. Involve helpers early rather than later in the process. Prepare. Plan but don't plan too much. When the moment is right, just do it!

14 – Enjoy life. Do the things that make you feel good. Express yourself. Sing. Dance. Play. Have fun. Laugh. Play some more. Do not worry too much about what other will think, and as long as you are not hurting anyone else, allow moments for the spontaneous manifestation of your free spirit. Jump up and down. Play the imaginary drums and guitar with a music that moves you. Exude joy. Surround yourself with positive, optimistic, and uplifting individuals who accept you as you are, friends who not only allow, but who encourage you to be yourself. Fill your days up with feel-good moments. More and more, do the things that make you feel good. Know that by doing the things that bring smiles to your face, you will attract more of them into your life.

<><><>

That's it.

I know I have given you good roots.

Now, open up your wings and fly.

Know that you are loved! Now and forever.

CHAPTER TWENTY THREE

REIKI-INSPIRED AFFIRMATIONS

The 5 Reiki Precepts

Just for today, I will be grateful.
Just for today, I will be fearless.
Just for today, I will be angerless.
Just for today, I will be honest.
Just for today, I will be kind.

I am a pure channel for loving Energy. The universal, intelligent, loving and healing Life Force Energy flows freely through me. It purifies me. It heals me. It protects me. It heals me physically, mentally, emotionally and spiritually.

My body is healthy.
My mind is clear.
My heart is joyful.
My soul is serene.

I am healed. I am healthy. I am protected. I am purified.

I am grateful.
I am free from fear.
I am free from anger.

I am honest.
I am kind.

I am whole. I am perfect. I am complete.

I am happy. I am healthy. I am wealthy. I am wise.

Love flows freely through me. I receive love and I give it. I give love and I receive it. Love flows and I glow.

I express gratitude all the time.
I live without fear.
I do not get angry.
I am honest with myself and others.
I am kind.

I am healed. I am healthy. I am protected. I am purified.

I am whole. I am perfect. I am complete.

I am happy. I am healthy. I am wealthy. I am wise.

I am grateful.
I am worry-free.
I am anger-free.
I am honest.
I am kind.

Today I am peaceful.
Gratitude pours out of my heart. I am grateful.
Fear and anxiety abandoned me. I am fearless.
Anger has no place in me. I embrace all situations and people without judgment.
Honesty lives in all my doings. I am honest.
Compassion and loving kindness are in all I do. I am loving and respectful.
~ Liz Velez

CHAPTER TWENTY FOUR

AN EPIPHANY OF ONENESS

I look around and see miracles all around me.
I look around and I see the Divine Presence everywhere, all around
me and in me.
I am part of the whole.
Actually I am not a part; I am the Whole.
I am
I don't exist isolated.
Separation is an illusion.
I am not this little, unconnected and detached being that I thought I
was.
I am the Whole.
I am
Only One exists.
I am the Universe.
I am the Immense One.
I am the Whole.
I am holy.
I am
I am everything that was, is and will be.
I am

I look around and see the Love manifesting itself everywhere.
The Divine Energy is everywhere.
I see the Divine Intelligence in the ocean, the air, the clouds, the sun,
the light, the birds, and even in a grain of sand.
Wind, water, earth, fire, all things are manifestations of the same
Divine Intelligence.
All things, and all persons everywhere are manifestations of this
Divine Intelligence.
Everything, everybody, everywhere, independent of time -- past,
present or future -- contains the same elements of this Divine
Presence.
Everything is a manifestation of this Divine Energy including you,
me, and everyone who has lived, is alive now, or is yet to be born.
I contain the same elements of the Divine Presence.
I am the Divine Presence.
I am the Divine Intelligence.
I am the Divine Energy.
I am Love.
I am.
And since I am the Divine Presence there is no reason ever to be
afraid, or worry about anything, not even death.
Physical death is just a trans-form-ation, a change of form.

Love runs freely through me.
It purifies me.
It heals me.
It protects me.
I receive Love.
I give Love.
I see Love all around me.
Love manifests itself everywhere.
Every single thing is a manifestation of the One Love.
I too am a manifestation of the One Love.
I am Love.
I am.

CHAPTER TWENTY FIVE

A REFLECTION ON MEDITATION

Meditation takes us to a resting place where we become able to recognize the Love – the beauty, intelligence, power, force and energy -- that exists all around us.

Meditation creates conditions to deeply experience the oneness of all, and feel that we are connected with everything else, and that each one of us is a part of the Whole.

Then, meditation takes us even further. It takes us beyond the feeling that we are just one part and leads us to understand that since all elements of the Whole are in us, we are the Whole.

Meditation allows us to conclude that there is no separation; that separation is an illusion. All the power resides in us already, and all we have to do is to allow Love – the beauty, intelligence, power, force and energy -- that already is within us, to come to light.

As we become better observers, we begin to see and feel the manifestation of the One Love everywhere.

We see that this manifestation is occurring spontaneously and effortlessly.

We then see ourselves as manifestations of that same Energy.

We reach the understanding that we have that Power.

We feel that we exude that Intelligence.

We feel that we express that Beauty.

We feel that the Force is with us.

We feel destined and perfectly capable of manifesting our uniqueness.

CHAPTER TWENTY SIX

FINDING YOUR OWN VOICE

We are, by nature, students and teachers. I am convinced that learning and teaching has no end and that we will be learning and teaching until the last moment of our physical existences and, who knows, even beyond.

I see evolution of consciousness as a never-ending journey.

In my attempts to learn and teach how to live a more joyful and fulfilling life, I have been blessed by the knowledge and wisdom of many amazing teachers who came before me. I read their books, listened to their recordings, watched their videos, attended their workshops, and experimented with the different practices they suggested. I recognize how tremendously important they were — and continue to be — in bringing me to where I am in my life, and I look forward to the amazing places they will be taking me in the future. They made and continue to make me better, and I am grateful to all of them.

Not only those who have written books that I have read, or facilitated classes that I have attended, were my teachers. My friends, especially those with whom I have deep conversations, have taught and continue to teach me a whole lot.

It is now very clear to me that we are all teachers to each other, and that everyone we meet can be a teacher to us, as long as we approach all situations with reverence and a sincere desire to learn.

The source from where lessons come is inexhaustible, and the flow of lessons is unstoppable, simply because abundance is the very nature of our world. With the constant progress in technology, more and more information is produced and made available to us.

Teachers keep showing up all the time: some of the lessons they bring are already known to us, some are improved versions of old lessons, and some are entirely new ones.

I consider that we are fortunate for having such easy access to all this wisdom, and I am grateful for that.

But the exposure to all this information, without clarity on how to process it, can become a source of bewilderment and anxiety.

We should realize that the amount of available information is already immense and will continue to grow without end. No one will ever be able to process all the information contained in all the good books, audio recordings, videos and courses that exist already, plus the ones that are coming out every day.

They are all good for our growth, but we should realize that too much of a good thing can be bad. Imagine, for instance, a reckless glutton who overindulges in eating. We shall not allow our insatiable hunger for knowledge — our desire to know it all — to drive us crazy.

A sane approach to processing information demands a few guidelines. Here are seven principles that serve me, and that I submit to your consideration, hoping they can serve you as well:

1 – Choose wisely.

Since there is more information available than you will ever be able to process, be selective. Consider that a lot of the life lessons are pretty much the same. Many times, what you think is new is just the same old lesson presented in a different way by the same teacher, or a new one. What you have to do is to ask yourself if what you are learning resonates with you. Does it excite you? Do you feel compelled to share it? Does it produce new insights? Does it help you move forward in your life? Does it make you better? If so, stick with it. These are all signs that you are receiving what you need at the stage of life you are currently in.

2 – Be aware of change, and release what doesn't serve you anymore.

We are constantly evolving. Maybe some beliefs and practices that made a lot of sense in the past, don't resonate with you anymore. That's OK. Let them go.

3 – Don't be judgmental.

Don't condemn others. Consider that wherever they are on their journeys is where they ought to be, and that, eventually, if it is to be so, they will see what you see, as you see. Look back and, if it is the case, say to yourself, "I too have been there and done that. I too have, in the past, believed what they believe now. It was good for me then, but it doesn't serve me anymore. What I know now, I didn't know then." Accept others wherever they may be, and gently help them to move on to better grounds, if they so desire.

4 – Don't be worried about what you don't know, or you think you don't know.

Don't consume yourself trying to know it all. Consider that you know more than enough already, and that what you need to do now is to ponder what you already know and put the good advice you have received to good use. Consider that whatever else you need to know will spontaneously come to you.

5 – Be aware of the difference between collecting information and exuding true knowledge.

Consider dedicating less time to the frantic collection of information and more time to calmly processing what you already have acquired. Don't satisfy yourself in remaining on the surface and being a mere regurgitator of someone else's ideas. Take time to go deeper, study, analyze, reflect, internalize the concepts learned, and make that knowledge your own. The widespread availability of good information is a good thing, but information alone, no matter how much of it is available, or how easy it may be to access, will not change our world. Only the diligent practice, by each one of us, of what is being taught by the masters will change minds, and this is what will change the world. The world changes when we change. Remember that only actions bring about results. Information alone will not bring about change. Change comes from action, so practice what you have learned.

6 – Be prepared to not follow anyone.

The true master will tell you, "Don't follow me. Stay with me for as long as you want, but know that the day will come when you will have to leave me, and I will have to leave you. That will be the day when you realize that the guide you have been waiting for has always been with you since the beginning. The sage is within you. The guru is you. Turn inward and get directions from the master who lives in you."

7 – Move your focus from the outside to the inside.

Stop looking for answers outside and begin finding them inside. Pay attention. Be alert. Know yourself. Find your own voice and speak your own authentic truth. From all the knowledge and wisdom that already resides within you, allow something new and beautiful to be born. Don't look back. Look forward. Envision the great days that are going to come. Bring out your unique messages to the world. Be of service to others and give your contribution to bring about a better world.

My spiritual teachers have taught me to seek in the silence, go within, and ask myself, over and over again, "Who am I?" They guided me to become the silent observer, the witness of the conversations taking place inside my head. They taught me how to slow down my hyperactive mind, and calmly stay in the here-now. Their command is clear: "Know yourself." Their instruction is clear: "Choose your thoughts carefully, because your thoughts create your life."

I can't deny that the works of great masters have taken me to higher levels of consciousness. Learning from them has been a great blessing, but I have realized that this journey is less about accumulation of information and knowledge, and more about my own intuitive and direct experience of who I am. More important than accumulating information is to continuously and sincerely ask myself…

Who am I?

What do I love?

How do I live knowing that I will die?

What are my gifts to the family of the Earth?

I have access to unlimited amounts of excellent information that keeps coming my way all the time, without interruption. But over and over again I was taught that the treasure I am seeking is not elsewhere; it is inside my own dwelling all the time.

So, at this stage of my life, I am trying to limit my exposure to external stimuli. The external stimulus that I am receptive to is the one that guides me to silently observe the internal chatter inside my hyperactive mind, the one that calms me down, and brings me to the peaceful center of my being where I can rest in the present moment.

I am turning inward and dedicating more of my time to hear, so I may speak with my own voice.

If this is the right time for you, then turn inward and find your own voice.

Namaste!

EPILOGUE

I prefer fluidity over rigidity. I prefer to follow my intuition than to follow inflexible plans. I prefer to experiment on my own -- and find out what works for me – over accepting without questioning what is handed down to me by authorities. I prefer to play than obey. That's the way I am, and not everyone is like me, I know. So, knowing the way I am, I want to close this book with this last advice…

Do Whatever Makes You Feel Good

Remember that what works for other people will not necessarily work for you. So, do whatever you want with the advice contained in this book, and in my other books and lectures as well. Get the techniques contained in this book and mix, combine, add, subtract, change, or even ignore them completely. Feel free to do whatever you want. Find out what works for you. Create your own method. Make it fun and exciting for you.

I myself started my journey with Centering Prayer in total silence. Then I added music in the background. Then I enjoyed many types of guided meditations. Then I began my Silent Peace Walks. And then I added Reiki in the mix. Meditation, Creative Visualization, Positive Affirmations, all together… It is a salad, and you know what? It is a delicious one. I love it. It is exciting. It is creative. It is fun. It makes me feel good!

Remember… Life is short.

Do Whatever Makes You Feel Good

Fill your life up with feel-good moments. Do more, everyday, of the things that make you feel good.

If you do so, you will be happy and you will make others, including me, very happy.

Remember…

"You are never given a wish without also being given the power to make it true."

Your grandest self and your best life are already here.

Get out of the way and allow them to come to light.

Allow.

Piero Falci

ADDITIONAL RESOURCES FOR YOUR JOURNEY

Here are some books that I encourage you to get acquainted with. They really helped me on my journey:

- Wishes Fulfilled: Mastering the Art of Manifesting – Wayne Dyer
- Manifest Your Destiny: Nine Spiritual Principle for Getting Everything You Want – Wayne Dyer
- Change Your Thoughts, Change Your Life: Living the Wisdom of the Tao – Wayne Dyer
- The Power of Intention: Learning to Co-create Your World Your Way - Wayne Dyer
- Creative Visualization - Shakti Gawain
- The Seven Spiritual Laws of Success - Deepak Chopra
- Spontaneous Fulfillment of Desire: Harnessing the Infinite Power of Coincidence to Create Miracles - Deepak Chopra
- You Can Heal Your Life - Louise Hay
- Meditation - Eknath Easwaran
- Zen Mind, Beginner's Mind - Shunryu Suzuki
- The Magic - Rhonda Byrnes

ABOUT THE AUTHOR

Piero Falci, the author of "Pay Attention! Be Alert! Discovering your Route to Happiness" and "Silent Peace Walk" is teacher who reflects about life, shares his insights, and inspires others.

He is a sought-after speaker, facilitator of workshops and retreats, and his blog, "Exploring and Inspiring," has a dedicated following.

With decades of experience as an instructor and coach, Piero has developed exceptional human relations skills that he successfully utilizes to engage, inspire, and motivate.

His workshops and retreats create opportunities for participants to pause, reflect and grow.

He teaches meditation, creative visualization, positive affirmations and other similar techniques that help individuals envision the life of their dreams, keep their commitments, and regularly do what is necessary to manifest their wishes.

Piero is passionate about helping others live happier and more fulfilling lives, and he brings this enthusiasm to his workshops and coaching sessions.

He was born and educated in Brazil, and after his college graduation, he continued his studies in Italy and Japan.

Besides English, he is fluent in Portuguese, Spanish and Italian.

He lived in Brazil and Argentina before settling in the United States.

For more information please visit:
- www.PieroFalci.com
- www.PieroFalci.com/blog

Piero@PieroFalci.com
954-914-1202

INVITE THE AUTHOR TO SPEAK

Piero Falci continues to spread his life-enhancing messages to all generations.

He is a dynamic and upbeat speaker who entertains and inspires individuals from all walks of life.

He speaks to all kinds of audiences, young and old, from business leaders to at-risk youth, from successful professionals to those facing the uncertainties of life.

His words give, to all of those going through critical moments in their lives, a renewed hope and energy to overcome their fears and face the challenges with a positive attitude.

Piero facilitates retreats, workshops, and team-building events.

Invite Piero to speak.

For more information please visit:
- www.PieroFalci.com
- www.PieroFalci.com/blog

Piero@PieroFalci.com
954-914-1202

FOLLOW YOUR BLISS
WORKSHOPS AND RETREATS

Do you feel that you need to take some time off to make an assessment of your life?

Do you feel it is time to seriously ponder, "Where am I? Where am I going? Where do I really want to be? What is calling me? Who am I meant to be?"

If you want to put yourself in motion to fulfill your life's purpose, we are here to help you.

If you are ready to heed your highest calling and follow your bliss, we are here to help you.

This is our mission and our commitment: to inspire you to take action and give you useful tools and resources that will help you bring about the life of your dreams.

Let us help you live the life of your dreams!

For more information please visit:
- www.PeacefulWays.org

GOAL-SETTING WORKSHOPS AND RETREATS

Are you discouraged because resolutions don't last? Do you abandon the pursuit of your life-changing goals rapidly? Do you think that this goal-setting thing doesn't work?

Join us for a time of renewal, reflection and goal-setting, and learn effective ways to access the power that will help you set and accomplish your goals.

Learn 3 powerful focusing techniques used by the most successful people in the world, techniques that will bring you back to your goals everyday, inspire you to take action everyday, and allow you to experience progress everyday.
· **Meditation**
· **Visualization**
· **Affirmation**

In a calm atmosphere, you will examine your life and uncover your most important goals. Since goal-setting is just the beginning of the process, during our time together you will also learn the JFT technique which will take you back to practice the techniques you learned on a regular basis. You will leave the workshop/retreat well equipped to go back to your goals and take action every single day, knowing that this is what will bring about the life you want to live.

Clear your mind, set goals, and get results!

Get the keys that will open doors for a better life!

For more information please visit:
- www.PeacefulWays.org

LEADERSHIP
COMMUNICATION
DIVERSITY AND INCLUSION
WORKSHOPS AND RETREATS

DAPA is a Training, Coaching and Consulting Services company that offers workshops on Leadership, Communication Skills, Diversity, Cultural Competency, and Sensitivity.

If you want to use the best practices of Leadership, Communications, and Diversity and Inclusion to improve attitudes and behaviors, increase commitment and loyalty, and unlock the full potential of your team, you came to the right place. Our successful training, coaching and consulting services will help you create a highly respectful, motivated, and productive work environment. If your goal is to enhance workplace harmony and overall productivity, contact us. We are here to partner with you.

Our goal is to put together and deliver the most effective programs for you and your teams. We always begin the process by doing a complimentary assessment interview to better understand your particular situation and expected outcomes. This understanding allows us to partner with you in designing the most effective courses of action, and customizing our programs to meet the particular needs of all stakeholders.

Please, feel free to contact us. Let us explore together what we can do for you and your workforce.

For more information please visit:
- www.DAPAdiversity.com
- www.DAPAdiversity.org

WORKSHOPS AND RETREATS
FOR
COUPLES AND PARENTS

Attention new parents!
A baby is about to arrive -- or has just arrived -- and you find yourselves asking, "Now, what? What are we going to do?" Have you thought about that? The arrival of a baby creates a perfect opportunity for couples to pause, reflect, and a launch a new start in life. Before you were just spouses, but now you are parents, and with this major change in your lives you must give yourselves some time to reflect on your new roles and the changes in your lives.

What kind of family do you want to create?
Our workshops are the perfect forums for you to entertain fundamental questions about your life, visualize the future, reach agreements with your partner, create a plan of action, and get motivated to implement it. During our workshops you will reflect on the parent -- and spouse -- you want to be, the children you want to raise, and the family you want to create. You will reflect on your own experiences, considering questions such as, "What have I learned from my parents? What was good and what was not so good about their parenting?" You will imagine the life and family of your dreams, practice techniques called Creative Visualization and Positive Affirmations, and leave the workshop with a plan of action to achieve your goals.

How are we doing as a family?
This workshop, which creates an opportunity for deep reflection, is good for all families, not only those with newborns. No matter your children's ages, it is always beneficial to pause and imagine the family you want to manifest. During this workshop you will also learn some simple but effective parenting and communication skills that will be useful to all family members for the rest of their lives.

Program:

- Assessing your current lifestyle and use of time.
- Reflecting on foreseeable lifestyle changes with the arrival of the new baby.
- Reflecting on your own trajectory and experiences.
- Reflecting on the type of family you want to have, the type of spouse and parent you want to be, and the type of children you want to raise and what you want for them.
- Learning and practicing effective parenting and communication skills
- Setting goals
- Learning to utilize Creative Visualization and Positive Affirmations
- Visualizing the future: your children, your spouse, your family, and you in 5, 10, 15, and 20 years from now.
- Reaching agreements and expressing personal commitments.
- Creating a Plan of Action.

You can create the family of your dreams!

Pausing, reflecting, and communicating is extremely important for anyone who wants to create a beautiful family. Our workshops create perfect opportunities to do just that.

Don't hesitate and enroll in this program now.

It will change your life!

For more information please visit:

- http://www.childbirthservicesflorida.com/parenting-for-new-parents.html

PEACEFUL WAYS

"Happiness is when what you think, what you say, and what you do are in harmony."

~ Gandhi

Peaceful Ways is an organization that exists to help people live better lives and, by doing so, make our world a better place for all.

We believe in helping individuals find their calling and purpose in life, and in supporting them in their efforts to remove the self-imposed obstacles that prevent them from being the best that they can be.

Gandhi's quote speaks volumes about what we have to do to achieve happiness: we must live out who we really are and bless the world with our uniqueness.

When we are authentic — when what we think, say and do are in harmony — love flows freely through us; the flow of giving and receiving intensifies, and we experience abundance.

Peaceful Ways is an educational organization that facilitates self-exploration, discovery and transformation, through workshops, retreats, and educational resources.

Let us help you live the life of your dreams!

For more information please visit:
- www.PeacefulWays.org

ONE PLANET UNITED

SILENT PEACE WALK

Piero Falci is the Program Director of One Planet United, a humanitarian organization dedicated to inspire people to "embrace diversity, promote unity, and create community."

He is the organizer and facilitator of a series of community-building and educational events, such as the Dialogues in Diversity where individuals from different backgrounds get together to learn more about one another, and "consciously unlearn the prejudices that they have unconsciously learned."

Piero is also in the organization's Board of Directors and Speakers Bureau.

Additionally Piero is the creator and leader of the "Silent Peace Walks."

For more information please visit:
- www.SilentPeaceWalk.org
- www.OPUnited.org

Piero@PieroFalci.com
954-914-1202

Made in the USA
Charleston, SC
18 October 2014